When We Were Colored

Colored

Clifton L. Taulbert

PENGUIN BOOKS

PENGUIN BOOKS
Published by the Penguin Group
Penguin Books USA Inc., 375 Hudson Street,
New York, New York 10014, U.S.A.
Penguin Books Ltd, 27 Wrights Lane, London W8 5TZ, England
Penguin Books Australia Ltd, Ringwood, Victoria, Australia
Penguin Books Canada Ltd, 10 Alcorn Avenue,
Toronto, Ontario, Canada M4V 3B2
Penguin Books (N.Z.) Ltd, 182–190 Wairau Road,
Auckland 10, New Zealand

Penguin Books Ltd, Registered Offices:
Harmondsworth, Middlesex, England

First published in the United States of America as *Once Upon a
Time When We Were Colored* by Council Oak Books 1989
Published in Penguin Books 1995

1 3 5 7 9 10 8 6 4 2

ISBN 0 14 02.4477 8
(CIP data available)

Printed in the United States of America
Set in Garamond Light
Designed by Karen Slankard

Dedicated to . . .

My son, Marshall Danzy
who thinks "colored" means crayolas.

My daughter, Anne Kathryn
who was born the day after I
made my first excerpt public reading.

My wife, Barbara Ann
who endured my early dawn writing habits.

My mother, Mary Taulbert
a strong lady with a definite sense of purpose.

The memory of my aunt,
Elna Peters Boose (Ma Ponk),
who raised me; an original colored lady.

My four sisters and two brothers:

Claudette
Clara
Carolyn
Connie
Claiborne
Johnny.

CONTENTS

Yazoo & Mississippi Valley Railroad Company.

LAND OFFICE.

No. _____

In Consideration of _____ Fifty six _____

cash in hand paid to it by _____ R J Jefferson _____ the _____
acknowledged, and the further sum of _____ Two hundred twenty _____
Dollars agreed to be paid as evidenced by the written obligation of said _____ R J _____
bearing even date herewith, whereby the said _____ R J Jefferson _____
YAZOO & MISSISSIPPI VALLEY RAILROAD COMPANY, or order, at the of _____
Ill., the sum of _____ Two hundred and twenty _____
in installments, with interest at _____ Seven _____ per cent, payable as follows:

WHEN DUE.	PRINCIPAL.	INTEREST.	WHEN DUE.
February 23rd 1895		1568	February 2
1897	4200	4372	
1899	5600	784	

The Yazoo & Mississippi Valley Railroad Company hereby _____
_____ the following lands situate _____
State of Mississippi, to-wit: _____ South west q _____
(SW¼ of NE¼) Section ten (10 _____
range eight (8) west _____
containing _____ Forty _____

To secure the prompt payment of the said sum of _____
together with the interest thereon as specified therein, and _____
to have the full force and effect of a mortgage, is hereby _____
this instrument conveyed.

This deed is made, delivered and accepted on the follow _____
If any taxes or charges on said lands shall remain u _____
holder of the written obligation hereby secured, may pay _____
cent per annum interest thereon, shall then and thereby _____
maturing.

The time of payment of the installments of principa _____
thereof, may be extended after default in the payment, a _____
shall bear interest at the rate of 10 per cent per annu _____
being also secured by the lien herein reserved.

All portions of the land hereinbefore described, if a _____
center of the railroad tracks of the grantor herein, and _____
tracks or right-of-way of the grantor herein, together _____
secure the main line, branches, side-tracks and embankm _____
expressly excepted from this conveyance and are not con _____

In the event default be made in the payment of any of th _____
security reserved and retained herein for the payment thereof _____
hereby reserves the right of entering upon the land conveyed _____
of the same. The grantor herein, or its assigns, are he _____
security has become impaired and possession of said land _____

Upon the failure to pay any one of said installmen _____
written obligation hereinbefore set forth, all of said inst _____
and a sale of the land hereby conveyed, or any part ther _____
money, and all taxes, interest and costs, by the said _____
principal door of the Court House of the said County _____
said sale being made at public outcry to the highest b _____
and terms of said sale, by posting a notice thereof at _____
aforesaid. At a sale of said land under the power of sa _____
assigns are hereby authorized and empowered to purchas _____
strangers to this conveyance, and in that event the auc _____
to make and deliver to the purchaser thereof a deed conv _____

In Testimony Whereof, The said Yazoo &

caused these presents to be signed by its Vice-President an _____
day of _____ February _____ 1894.

YAZOO _____

ATTEST:

_____ SECRETARY.

_____ LAND-COMMISSIONER.

NOTICE TO OWNERS OF LANDS SOLD FOR TAXES

To _____ Sidney Williams _____
% Phillis Williams ho _____

Issued _____ 1-31 _____ 19 _____
_____ W P Kimbrey _____ Clerk.

By _____ D. C.

Received by me, this _____ day of _____
_____ 19 _____

_____ Sheriff.

Returned _____ County
this _____ 19 _____
_____ Clerk.
_____ D. C.

NOTICE TO OWNERS OF LANDS SOLD FOR TAXES

To _____ Sidney Williams _____
% Phillis Williams ho _____

Issued _____ 1-31 _____ 19 35
_____ W P Kimbrey _____ Clerk.

By _____ D. C.

Received by me, this _____ day of _____
_____ 19 _____

_____ Sheriff.

Returned _____ executed and filed
this _____ day of _____ 19 _____
_____ Clerk.
By _____ D. C.

STATEMENT OF TAXES, COSTS AND FEES

Taxes and Costs	$ 1065
_____ per cent Damages	$ 2562
Tax of 19 32	$ 966
Tax of 19 33	$ 13370
Tax of 19 34	$ 70
Five per cent Damages	$ 363
Clerk's Fee for Redemption	$ 763
Total	$ 350
Clerk's Fee for Issuing Notice	$ 75
Sheriff's Fee for Serving Notice	$ 150
Total Due	$ 3746

HEDERMAN BROS. JACKSON, MISS.

Introduction

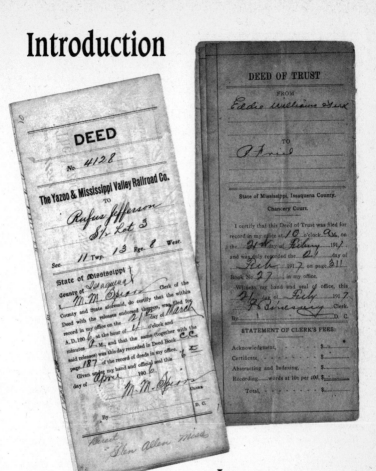

It was a beautiful October day in the 1970s. It was not quite like those other October days when I was a child growing up in this southern cotton community, but it was beautiful nonetheless. I had come home for my yearly pilgrimage to see Glen Allan, Mississippi, to remember the life I once knew and visit my older relatives. Somehow I always felt better after visiting those tired old people who had given me strength when I was a child. So many changes had taken place in Glen Allan. "Colored" people were now "black," soap operas had replaced quilting bees in their homes, and the schools their children attended were now integrated. But the land was the same; the rich delta land had not changed. And the cotton smelled as it did in the early '50s when I picked it as a way of life. Now, however, the quarter of a mile long cotton rows seemed shorter and instead of the bent backs and scratched hands of hundreds of coloreds picking cotton, there were scores of big red machines harvesting the white fields. As always, the land was giving life, being faithful, fruitful and productive, providing stability and a sense of worth.

I made it a point to visit my old aunt, Mozella Alexander. She insisted I sit and listen as she vividly recalled the times when her grandparents owned a plantation five miles from Glen Allan — a plantation they called Freemount. As we sat in her shotgun house that was falling on one end and propped up on the other, she rocked, swatted flies and told me all about old man Sidney Williams, Miss Phoebe, Rosa Morgan, Tom Williams and the rest that were known at the turn of the century as "the big colored landowners."

As she talked, her smooth black face shone with a pride that I don't know if I'll ever possess. "Son, my pa and your great-great grandpa were somebody. Oh chile, they had plenty land, mules, hogs and chickens and jest 'bout eberthang."

She talked with increasing excitement. Even though she was renting a run-down house, she knew that she was descended from the colored landed gentry. I guess that's why she was labelled "uppity." Even at her age she walked straight as an arrow.

"All out dar in de colony was colored when I wuz a chile. Yez sir my ole grandpa worked dat land like it was no t'morrow."

I knew the land she spoke of, although Freemount no longer existed. It was near the colored colony, a large parcel of land which I'd also heard was once in my family. I remember some of the older people saying, "Chile y'all folks shore had some land out dar in de colony." But for some reason those sayings never reached my belly. Land ownership and the sense of worth it brings seemed to have died out during my parents' time. I responded to this story as if it might be colored folklore. All my life most of the land owners had been white. When I'd go to the colony, it was their stately homes I'd see first. It never dawned on me that these houses, so seemingly permanent on their sites, were not the beginning. Little did I know they were built upon the sweat and blood of a different set of landowners, black men and women who tamed the land and gave it such an appropriate name, "Freemount."

Aunt Mozella talked for hours and I listened politely. At last I attempted to take my leave, but she stopped me.

"Set down, son. Lemme give ya something. And you hold onto it. It's valuable. No matter what happened to me, I'se always held onto these."

She got up and walked over to a trunk that was probably twice her age. She was old, colored and proud, with not a wrinkle in her cinnamon face. As she bent over her trunk and undid the double locks, I looked around at her tattered home, wall papered with pages from the Sears catalog. I wondered what of value she could possibly give me, her educated grand nephew.

Turning from the trunk she stood in front of me holding in her black hands a bundle of papers tied securely with old rags. Her cinnamon face shone as she pressed the papers to my hands.

"Here son, take 'em. Hold 'em. Yessir, here's de proof. It's all here. All dat my grandaddy worked for is right here."

I would later learn that in that moment, she had released to my generation the legal proof of our family's land ownership. All I had heard as a child was true.

I stood there at the foot of her iron bed holding the ancient papers. I'd been led to believe that coloreds never kept their papers. Nervously I untied the bundle and unfolded the fragile deeds. I was holding not the copies but the actual documents signed in ink by my great-great-grandfathers Sidney Williams and Ben Morgan, and the land commissioner for the State of Mississippi. Almost a century later these deeds spoke to me from their faded pages and verified for all time to come that Freemount had once really existed.

My discovery of these deeds affected me oddly. All my life, growing up in the colored section of the little Mississippi town of Glen Allan, I had been taught to respect the owners of the large plantations. In the agrarian South, land ownership more than any other factor decided who had status; the more land a person owned, the more he was worth. The realization that I was the descendant of black plantation owners gave me a sudden sense of pride. At the same time I felt cheated. The land which should have been my birthright had been lost, taken from my family during the Depression, sold without my great grandparents' knowledge at a tax auction for money they'd never known they owed. I'd grown up in the '50s, under a system of segregation which enforced on all people of my race an inferior status — a sense of worthlessness which was wholly illegitimate, but which I had striven all my life to overcome.

On further reflection, I realized that many of the values of the Southern culture had been illegitimate, even, perhaps, the value placed on land ownership. For the truth is, man cannot really own the land; we are only trustees for a time. Eventually the land will claim us and we'll return to our mother earth. Knowing this gives me some solace as I look at antiquated deeds dated in the late 1800s and signed over to my great-great-grandparents by the vice-president of the Yazoo and Mississippi Valley Railroad Company and its land commissioners. This land, once called Freemount, has probably had more trustees and names than we'll ever know.

If land ownership is not a legitimate measure of a people's worth, I wondered, what is? I began to think about my childhood and other values I'd learned as I grew up in an environment much like that experienced by thousands of other colored Americans. Even though segregation was a painful reality for us, there were some very good things that happened. Today I enjoy the broader society in which I live and I would never want to return to forced segregation, but I also have a deeply-felt sense that important values were conveyed to me in my colored childhood, values we're in danger of losing in our integrated world. As a child, I was not only protected, but also nourished, encouraged, taught, and loved by people who, with no land, little money and few other resources, displayed the strength of a love which knew no measure. I have come to believe that this love is the true value, the legitimate measure of a people's worth.

I was barely seventeen when I left my childhood home in Glen Allan and boarded the Illinois Central north to Saint Louis and into the 1960s, which would forever change the fabric of our society. Today my children are growing up in a world where "color" is something that comes in a box of crayons — a world of Bill Cosby and Yves St. Laurent. I have written *Once Upon A Time When We Were Colored* because I want my children to know of the life-style that gave them their father and their mother. It is very difficult to master the present and make a meaningful contribution to the future unless you understand and appreciate the past. In our desire as black Americans to put segregation behind us, we have put ourselves in danger of forgetting our past — the good with the bad. I believe that to forget our colored past is to forget ourselves, who we are and what we've come from.

This book is not the story of Freemount and the years when blacks owned the land. It is the story of a mostly landless people, the coloreds, who lived in Glen Allan and other small southern towns during the last years of segregation. I have written it to recall a treasure more valuable and enduring than land ownership. It is the treasure that stood out in my colored childhood when there was so little else, and it has been a source of strength to me in all the years since then. That treasure is the nourishing love that came to me from my extended family of aunts, uncles, parents, grandparents, great-grandparents, cousins, neighbors and friends. Rich in love, this congregation of black maids, field hands and tenant farmers worked the cotton fields, fished Lake Washington, gathered at St. Mark's Missionary Baptist Church to sing and pray, and gathered at the Greenville train station to bid farewell to loved ones moving north. In ordinary daily living through very difficult times, they showed themselves to be a great people. They are the reason I want today's world to remember an era that in our haste we might mistakenly forget — that era when we were called colored.

Chapter One

Poppa, Black Buddha of the South

Long ago
when southern
plantations
were plentiful
and colored
sharecroppers still dreamed and the agrarian South was
making a significant contribution to the gross national prod-
uct, small southern towns were springing up almost daily
with designs on becoming southern ladies of commerce.
Glen Allan, Mississippi, was such a place and was physically
positioned to achieve that goal. And although she had much

of what was required — a long lazy flowing lake framed with towering cypress trees and cypress stumps, mansions with white imposing columns that seemed to reach for the sky — she never quite became the lady. She remained a country girl with a few southern charms that would hold our attention while we called her our hometown.

Growing up as a young colored boy in Glen Allan, I didn't pay much attention to her lack of industry or the slow decline of cotton as king. I just lived for Saturdays when Poppa would take me to Greenville, the Queen City of the Delta, where we would buy hot French bread and frozen custard ice cream.

When I think of Poppa today, I am reminded of a colored southern Buddha. He was robust, very imposing and his head was as clean and shiny as that of an ancient Chinese god. Being a well-known and respected Baptist preacher, he was looked to for his wisdom and in many instances served as a go-between for the coloreds when problems arose involving whites. You could always count on Elder Young. I was too young to appreciate his intervention, but I was old enough to understand and feel his love for me, his great-grandson. And every Saturday morning during the summer and early fall, I could look forward to joining Poppa for our traditional ride to Greenville.

Poppa and I were very close. I had been born in his house, as were my mother and her mother before her. My mother was unmarried and just out of high school when I came into this world, and when she later married, it was felt that I would be better off living with Poppa and his wife Ma Pearl. Even though I was not raised by my mother, she lived within walking distance of Poppa's house. I spent a great deal of time with her as well as with my other aunts and uncles, enjoying the benefits of an extended family. By the time I was five, Ma Pearl had become too sick to take care of me and I went to live with my great-aunt, Ma Ponk. Over the years, my relationship with Poppa continued to grow even though I had gone to live with Ma Ponk. I built my world around Poppa and he protected me from the harsher realities of our complex social environment.

Poppa was more than my best friend; he was also the essence of Christmas. For colored children in Glen Allan, Christmas was the only time of year we got fresh fruit and toys. We each got one toy at Christmas, and today it seems amazing how those toys would last forever — or at least 364 days until Christmas came again. December 24 was a big night for us, and we didn't care whether Santa Claus was white, green or yellow, just as long as he came down our chimney. Poppa always made sure that something special happened in our lives at Christmas. We'd go around to his house early on Christmas morning and he'd have eggnog and bowls and bowls of fresh apples and oranges and pecans and walnuts — all the things that we rarely saw during the rest of the year. On Christmas it seemed we stepped into a fantasy land of new toys and good food, and Poppa was at its center.

Getting to go to Greenville with Poppa on a Saturday morning was almost as exciting as Christmas. I'd be up early in the morning, long before seven o'clock. I didn't want to miss the Saturday trip. I'd grab the car rags from the screened porch and a broom from the storehouse and I'd do my best to clean the old '49 Buick that served as a small field car during the week. I would work hard to get a good shine on the outside and all the field dirt from the inside. I was going to Greenville, and I couldn't wait. Poppa would never be ready as quickly as I expected him. He would always take his time.

Impatient to go, I'd ease into the front room, where Poppa would be putting the finishing touches on his shaving. He shaved his face and head every day. There he'd sit in the big black leather parlor chair by the door to the small bedroom, sharpening his razor on the long razor strops hung by the door. I would watch in complete silence as the long blade of the razor, expertly handled, removed all signs of hair from his face and head. Afterwards Poppa would rub alcohol all over his scalp with a hot towel, then he would rub oil over his face and head, creating the shiny image of Buddha that I had come to love. With the shaving complete, I knew it wouldn't be long. Poppa would put on his best white shirt and black suit. He'd chain his gold pocket watch across his belly, then get his hat. While he was finishing this careful process of dressing, I sat on the tall steps that led to the front porch. With my arms wrapped around my knees that were bent up to my chin, I would just sit and look as far as I could see. And my eyes could see no farther than Greenfield, a series of cotton farms and sharecroppers' homes. Because I could see no farther, I always thought Greenfield was the end of my world. I knew the colored colony was behind Greenfield, but I didn't understand why I couldn't see it. The colony was mostly colored, a self-sufficient community established by blacks after the Civil War and expanded through the purchase of land from the Illinois Central Railroad.

At the screech of the screen door behind me, I jumped up and looked into Poppa's face. There he stood with his hat in his hand and his ever-present pipe in his mouth. Together we walked down the steps from the front garret (as he called the porch) to the '49 Buick parked by the side of the house. Poppa got in and turned the key. The Buick never would start, however, until Poppa got out again, raised the hood and did some tinkering. Usually the tinkering didn't work either, and Poppa, as a last resort, would always hit something under the hood with a chinaberry stick. Then the motor would leap to life and we'd back out of the yard and head toward Greenville.

As we drove slowly up the road, Poppa would stop and talk with his friends. Being young, I could only wait impatiently. I remember that one of the people Poppa regularly stopped to pick up was Mr. Louis Fields.

Mr. Louis was one of the few hitchhikers I enjoyed. He and his wife, Miss Sarah, were my unofficial godparents. Not only was he the best of listeners, but Miss Sarah was a wonderful cook. They lived on the back side of Glen Allan in a large rambling sharecropper's house that they rented from Miss Spencer, the white lady who owned most of the land in our town. Their house was once bright green with a shiny tin roof, but time had peeled the paint, and the rain and sun had dulled and rusted the old roof. On those days when I ate with the Fieldses, I loved visiting and sitting on the big back porch while Miss Sarah cooked. I answered Mr. Louis' questions about what I wanted to be when I grew up while the smell of Miss Sarah's cured ham and candied sweet potatoes made my stomach growl.

Dressed in his starched khakis, white shirt, highly polished shoes and chewing his long cigar, Mr. Louis would take the wash pan out to the pump and fill it with water. Then we'd wash up and within minutes, we'd be ready to eat. We'd shoo flies and talk as we ate; Mr. Louis would tell me that I could be anything I wanted to be.

"Go all the way, boy, study hard, learn to draw buildings, be a doctor, do good in school; ain't nothing to field work."

He talked, I ate, he talked, I listened. Miss Sarah never said too much. She just cooked, kept her house spotless and kept Mr. Louis neatly dressed all the time. After finishing our food, Mr. Louis would prepare to take a nap and I would be sent home. They moved from Glen Allan before I grew up, but the "big shot" — as he was called because of how he dressed and his conversations of dreams — always inquired about my progress in school. On those mornings when Poppa and I were headed for Greenville in the old Buick, he'd always stop to carry Mr. Louis uptown.

While they talked I sat quietly, counted my money and visualized the frozen custard I was going to get in Greenville. Even though the distance from Poppa's house to the main street uptown was less than one mile, Poppa's slow driving and periodic stops made it seem longer. Mr. Louis would only want to go as far as Mount Zion Church, so Poppa would let him out, and proceed to the main road — until he was stopped by Preacher Hurn.

Preacher Hurn was from the colored colony and came to Glen Allan every Saturday. It didn't matter that we were on our way to the city; he always wanted to discuss a major Bible issue and, because of a speech impediment, it took him an abnormal amount of time to get his points across. Poppa was patient, but he kept the motor running while he talked to

Preacher Hurn. The preacher's favorite question centered around the date of Christ's return. Poppa, though a good preacher himself, was no match for Preacher Hurn's knowledge. Preacher Hurn was committed to the ministry but had no church of his own. He spent many hours reading Bible sources preparing himself for his eventual election to a church, a call that never came.

Poppa quietly assured Preacher Hurn that the return would not be tomorrow. Not one to give up easily, Preacher Hurn pointed to the advent of the skywriting airplane as an example that the end of time was fast approaching. Poppa knew from experience that he had better think and answer quickly if we were ever to get to Greenville. Once Preacher Hurn got started, there was the danger that we'd be sitting there still discussing the end times when the eastern skies split and the final trumpet call resounded.

"Preacher Hurn, God's coming but we won't figure it out today. We are going to Greenville now. I'll talk more when I git back later on dis evenin'."

Poppa's firmness and the raised sound of the engine convinced Preacher Hurn to let us go. Mumbling under his breath, Poppa slowly started the trip again. I sat comfortably on the front seat, dangling my legs that almost reached to the floor, while recounting my money and mentally purchasing more and more frozen custard. Poppa kept humming a verse of song, "Don't let that evening sun go down," as he drove past the quarters. He paused just a bit to honk the horn at Mr. Cape and Miss Bessie Ann. No matter the day or night, they'd always be sitting on their front porch, talking with folks strolling by and waving at those driving by. Most of the houses in the quarters looked just alike, two rooms and a small front porch, serviced by an outdoor toilet. But Miss Bessie Ann and Mr. Cape, good friends to our family, had added warmth to their rather plain surroundings by hanging a swing on the front porch and planting morning-glory vines on the west side. Miss Bessie Ann had also planted a few sunflowers in the front. Poppa and I waved as we went past. We were approaching uptown and Allan Chapel AME Church, which stood at the edge of the colored section.

Allan Chapel was one of the more impressive of the colored churches in Glen Allan because of its traditional AME styling and the fact that presiding elders came from faraway cities to monitor the activity of the church. I can't remember much about Allan Chapel except that a number of the colored teachers attended and Ma Ponk always complained that "not much spirit could be felt there." I knew they sang out of books, and no one shouted or got overcome with grief during their services. Maybe that's what was meant by a lack of spirit. Spirited or not, Allan Chapel was an integral part of the Glen Allan colored community, and it always reminds me of Miss Mary Maxey, one of our best-known colored teachers, a devoted member of her Methodist church. She was always a teacher, seven days a week, speaking correctly, dressing properly and correcting the many young colored boys and girls in our town.

As we neared Allan Chapel I heard Poppa mention the need for gas. Allan Chapel was at the intersection, so Poppa stopped and made sure the oncoming car of whites had the right-of-way. Secure that it was our turn, Poppa continued the slow drive toward the Standard Oil station. Now we were uptown.

Even though it was just one single street developed on the east side of beautiful Lake Washington, "uptown" was our center of commerce. In Glen Allan, the stores uptown were pretty much nationalized. There was the Italian meat market, Tony's; there was T. Y. Quong's, the "Chinese" store; and there was Mr. Carr's store, which was the "white" store. Mr. Freid's hardware store and Mr. Jake Stein's grocery store were referred to as the "Jewish" stores. Miss Maxey, when she wasn't teaching school, worked for Mr. Freid. In fact, she was one of the first colored people to wait on white customers. All of the prices in Mr. Freid's were written in Hebrew. Ma Ponk said that was on purpose, so no one would know what things cost and the store could charge more to the coloreds and less to the whites.

Poppa waved at Miss Hester, the Freids' cook, who was coming out of Mr. Jake Stein's grocery store, and then stopped to ask Miss Hester if she needed a ride over to the Freids' house, which was uptown by the town park. Miss Hester acknowledged Poppa, but assured him that she didn't. Dressed in her starched white cook's uniform, she looked as white as the Freids. Everyone knew that she was almost white and those who didn't know would soon learn; Miss Hester religiously pointed out that with just a few more pints of her father's blood, she'd be all white. When she wore her hair down, one would tend to agree with her.

We passed the Dixie Theater, a one-room white block building that provided the town's entertainment. Going to the Dixie was a rare treat for me. According to Ma Ponk, good colored folk did not spend much time there. If it weren't for the fact that Ma Ponk could sit on Miss Bessie Ann's front porch, which was near uptown, and wait for me, I might never have had the chance to go to the Dixie.

"Poppa, I thank I gotta go peepee."

"Hold it, boy, till we get the gas and get outta town."

I held my little legs tightly together while we drove past the park, where coloreds weren't allowed. Poppa slowed down briefly to talk with Aunt Lurlean as she was coming out of the Chinaman's store. According to Ma Ponk, Aunt Lurlean's sister, she'd spend every dime she made with T. Y. Her arms were loaded with bags of canned goods, but she stopped for a moment, came around to the side of the car and patted me on my head as she gave Poppa some money to bring her a wide-brimmed straw hat from Greenville. Aunt Lurlean was among the light colored women, and the wide-brimmed sun hat would keep her face from too much sun. I didn't say much. Between having to pee and wanting to get to Greenville, I was totally preoccupied. At last Poppa said goodbye to Aunt Lurlean, and we drove on past the drugstore, the post office and Mr. Youngblood's Department Store. The loafers' bench, as the yellow bench in front of the drugstore was called, was filled with colored people waiting on the bus. Poppa knew them all. Some he pastored, others he had gotten out of trouble.

We drove on past Dr. Duke's house by the lake and Miss Knight's house and seamstress shop next to it. Once past the white Baptist church, we could see and hear the activity of the local Standard gas station.

"Gotta get gas," mumbled Poppa as he pulled in. "Cliff, you set up, shet up. You ain't no nigger," he said as he rolled down the window.

"What can I do for you, preacher?" asked the white attendant as he spit out his snuff and wiped his mouth with a red calico handkerchief.

"A dollar fifty worth of regular, Mr. Bob," Poppa said as he gave me the eye.

"Ya'll going to the city to spend the money, huh, preacher? Well, don't git in no trouble," the attendant routinely said as he finished pumping the gas and getting his money.

"Much obliged to you, Mr. Bob." Poppa grinned as he rolled up the window. He drove away mumbling under his breath, "Who do that cracker think he is?"

I reminded Poppa that I had to pee real badly. I knew not to ask to use the toilet at the station. More than once I had been told about the importance of observing the "white only" signs.

"Hold it just a little longer, boy. We'll be up here by a field in no time."

Poppa had to drive slowly for the first quarter of a mile from the station, because we'd be passing Miss Spencer's mansion. In addition to her being a white woman, she was known as a reckless driver, and we had the responsibility to ensure that if she came out of her driveway in her Duesenberg without stopping, she'd have plenty of room. Even though I had never been inside her house, I had been to her back door with Ma Mae, my aunt, a well-known and respected colored cook. It was Gothic in style, not like the traditional southern mansions, but a showplace nonetheless. Significant to me was the fact that her mansion had been built in part by my great-great-grandfather Saul Peters and his brothers. According to Ma Ponk and cousin Savannah, Grandpa Saul and his brothers left Demopolis, Alabama, in the 1800s and moved to the Mississippi Delta as part of an artisan team of carpenters that specialized in the building of the famed southern antebellum homes. The Peters brothers, as they were known, applied their carpentry skills to the building of their own homes as well. Poppa's house (which was the original home of Grandpa Sidney Peters) was a classic example of their skills. Whereas most of our relatives and neighbors lived in the traditional shotgun houses, I recall Poppa's as a large rambling house with separate bedrooms, a formal dining and living room with two screened-in sun rooms. We certainly did not have the elegance of Miss Spencer's mansion, but we enjoyed the talents of some of the South's best carpenters.

Poppa drove past the mansion, relieved not to encounter Miss Spencer in her Duesenberg. Within minutes we'd see the white Methodist church, Wildwood Plantation and the famed Linden Plantation that was established by General Wade Hampton after the Civil War. As we slowly passed the places we both knew so well, we kept looking for a field with an accessible turn road.

Just past the Linden Plantation, we came to a small dirt road south of Daniel Chapel AME Church. Poppa pulled off the old Number 1 Highway. I jumped out very quickly and stood on the side of the car not facing the road where I relieved myself in a steady stream against the weeds. Then we were really on our way. Poppa hummed his favorite hymn and I counted my money as we rolled toward Greenville.

We passed scores of small plantations outlined by small shotgun houses filled with colored faces. Poppa would honk his horn and wave, but to my relief he kept driving. Maybe it was the never-ending rows of oil-soaked electric poles and the constant hum of the old Buick, but I soon fell asleep with my nickels held tightly in my fist.

"Wake up, boy, wake up. We here," Poppa nudged.

As I raised up to look around me, Poppa was busy trying to find a parking space down by the levee. After Poppa put his pennies in the meter, he'd grab my hand and together we'd walk down the street to the bakery and the frozen-custard stand. Because I was so fascinated by the crowd, Poppa would jerk my hand to remind me of "my place." I was so excited to get to the frozen-custard stand that I hardly watched where I was walking. But he would pull me up just in time so we could step aside and let the white people pass. Poppa would tip his hat and hold me closely by his side until the white people were clearly in front of us. Secure in the grip of Poppa's calloused hands, I never stopped smiling, because I could see the frozen-custard stand. I had not a care in the world as I purchased my double cone of frozen custard. Holding it in one hand while Poppa's strong grip held my other, I was totally contented. My world was complete and colored.

With frozen custard dripping from my mouth, I walked with Poppa a little farther to the bakery. We could smell hot French bread all the way up the street.

"That long piece of French bread, please, sir," Poppa asked the baker as we both inhaled the yeasty smells of the bakery.

"Anything else, preacher?" the baker asked, handing us the wrapped package. Reaching out to accept our money, the baker made sure his white hands did not touch Poppa's strong colored ones. Once outside, this man I loved began to break the hot loaf into small pieces, and we ate as we walked back to the levee. Poppa with his French bread and I with the last of my frozen custard walked down Washington Avenue hand in hand.

Poppa would complete the rest of his errands and visit a few friends. Then we'd begin the trip home to Glen Allan. I would settle in for a long nap as my Saturday ended and Poppa hummed, "That evenin' sun is setting fast."

Chapter Two

Long Brown Stockings and Colored Debutantes

Mama and I left Poppa's house early on that Monday morning because we both had to walk to Peru school, the plantation school where she taught. It was a long hot walk with no chance for a ride because there weren't many cars in the colored section. I was not yet five years old and more of a burden than a blessing, but Mama had nowhere to leave me because all my aunts were field workers during the day. So I went with her every day and sat in the back of the old plantation church which served as the schoolhouse.

There weren't many colored plantation schoolhouses left by the time I was born. Prior to my birth, during my mother's maturing years and those of her parents, one-room plantation schools were the primary source of education for colored children growing up in and around small southern towns. Even though Mama had barely graduated from high school at the time, she was considered a capable teacher.

In spite of her lack of college training Mama was creative and concerned. It didn't matter to her that the Peru school was miles from her house and that she had to teach all eight grades in one room. She was dedicated, and her students, many close to her age, called her Miss Mary. Mama especially enjoyed teaching in the spring when the old unpainted colored Baptist church would be surrounded by green meadows and deep ravines with ropes and ropes of long green vines. The springtime also made our long walk easier.

Mama always sought ways to get her students' parents involved. For instance, the parents took turns bringing and serving the school lunch. Everyone at the school was poor except the Crockett children; their father was the colored overseer at the plantation. The rest of the sharecropping and tenant families had very little money, so when my mother asked that they assist in providing and serving the food, she made it clear that they could bring whatever they had. And that they did. Each day there was a variation of beans, peas and cornbread or peas, okra, beans and cornbread. The food was plain, but hot and tasty. It was free, and it was much better than the previous school lunch, which was none.

The ladies would get permission to leave the fields a little early and while Mama was teaching, they'd be getting the old iron stove hot. These field hands-turned-volunteer-cooks would heat the beans on the stove and turn one of the long church benches into a table to serve the hot meal.

For nearly a year I walked to Peru school with my mother and watched her try to bring education to young people who were being raised to be plantation workers in a society where planting and harvesting of cotton took precedence over the cultivation of minds.

Even though the plantation schools were ill-equipped and little was provided to facilitate education, I always enjoyed watching my mother take the ordinary and make it something special. For instance, Mama would get all the farm families involved in creating the annual Peru School Christmas pageant. One year, with the help of a few faithful parents, Mama turned the altar area of the church into Bethlehem. Dried cotton stalks became stubble for the manger floor and hand-cut logs made up the exposed beams that framed the stable. Sheets and multicolored quilts formed the walls of a Jewish inn, and the children of tired field hands became angels, shepherds and kings. The families crowded into the one-room building, their greased faces shining as they watched their children perform. I remember parents crying as the children recited their lines by memory. Then the entire audience joined in as Doris Crockett, one of the angels, led them in singing "Silent Night."

As the years went by and minor incidents of progress came our way, the plantation schools would pass away and the separate-but-equal policy would be established, paving the way for the central colored schools that served not only the small towns of their location but also the surrounding plantations.

Finally it was time to start my education at the colored school in Glen Allan. I wasn't six, but I had been given permission to start school early. Miss Maxey was the teacher, the principal, and the disciplinarian. She was also a good friend with my mother, Ma Ponk, and Mama Pearl. I was excited, my mother was overjoyed and Ma Pearl was determined that her great-grandson would start his first day warmly dressed and supplied with adequate food.

The fall school term always coincided with the time between the end of cotton-chopping season and the start of cotton-picking season. This brief pause gave the parents a chance to buy winter clothes and get their children ready for school. For those children whose parents were tenant farmers or sharecroppers, their school cycle revolved around the needs of the farms or plantations. I was fortunate in that my folks were not sharecroppers. We lived in town, which gave me full opportunity to go to school. Getting an education was a priority in our house. After all, Poppa — Elder Young — was a well-known Baptist preacher.

On that long-awaited September day, I got up early. I didn't want to be late, and I wanted to walk with all the other children. Poppa was already up having his coffee, and Mama Pearl as usual was busy as a colored bee in her kitchen.

A new day — a first day — and new clothes! School was going to be fun. As I was getting up, I looked around, but I couldn't find my new clothes.

"Mama Pearl, where's my clothes?"

"Boy, don't be so hurried, come on out here on the sun porch and eat your breakfast. I laid out your clothes on the bed in my room."

I put my plaid robe over the pajamas which Mama Pearl made me wear summer and winter and went out to have breakfast with Poppa. Poppa was a great preacher but he was not much at talking while eating, and I was so excited about school that I just ate a few mouthfuls of grits and cured ham before I ran into the small bedroom to get dressed.

There, laid out on the big brass bed, were my new school clothes. I stood motionless looking at them stunned and embarrassed. Next to my new blue jeans lay two awful pieces of clothing — a pair of ugly brown knee-high stockings and a suit of white flannel long johns. Determined to keep me warm, Mama Pearl had also bought me a new pair of high-topped shoes. Even at the tender age of five I knew everyone would laugh at me in these clothes. I would be the only kid dressed head to toe by a great-grandmother who cared nothing about the boxer shorts, short socks and low-quartered shoes all the other children would be wearing.

Embarrassed, but determined to live through it, I dressed and waited for Mama Pearl to fix my lunch. We lived only four houses from the school, but it was against the rules for students to come home for lunch. While she was in the kitchen, I went out on the porch, where I hurriedly rolled my long johns up to my knees and my brown stockings down into the sides of my high-topped shoes. I was determined not to be laughed out of school with my long johns and brown stockings showing.

I could hear them coming down the gravel road, all my friends and cousins, laughing and talking, and I could hardly wait to join the big kids on my way to school. I started for the door but was intercepted by Mama Pearl. She came out from the kitchen and handed me my lunch. Then, as she placed a green corduroy cap on my head, pulled the flaps down over my ears and buckled the strap securely under my chin, she also gave me a long list of don'ts:

"Don't sass Miss May Maxey."

"Don't leave the school ground."

"Don't be cutting up at yore seat."

"And come straight home after school is out."

"Yes'm," I replied to each one, but I knew that all her don'ts would turn out to be my friends' dos. Towering over me, Mama Pearl, a big woman with red hair and freckles, kept giving me instructions as my friends called me to join them. While I stood there under the iron finger of love, I looked out into the street at the other boys. Unlike me, they wore no caps. They all had low-quartered shoes and they were throwing rocks and hitting dogs. I almost wished that they'd leave me and let me walk alone. But no such luck. Instead, Mama Pearl raised her voice high enough to let them hear her list of don'ts as they waited for me in the street. At last she finished and I was free to join them.

Having gotten my head covered, my molasses bucket filled with food, and my body wrapped in long johns and stockings,

Mama Pearl was satisfied that I would not get pleurisy and that I was ready to learn. She stood on the top step, hands on her hips, determined not to move until I was out of eyesight.

As we passed Miss Martha Clinton's place and Mr. George Stanley's shotgun house, I could relax and join the group. I was now out of Mama Pearl's range. Suddenly, however, all the boys wanted to see what was in my Br'er Rabbit Molasses lunch bucket. The bigger boys jerked on my bucket as I held onto it and tried to run. By the time they finished jerking and I finished running, my flap jacks, molasses and salt-meat strips were mangled together. The bigger boys didn't seem to mind, however. They quickly opened my bucket and ate my food.

I arrived at school carrying an empty bucket. When lunch time came I was hungry. I cried to go home, and Miss Maxey gave me permission. With tears streaming down my round colored face, I ran as fast as I could to Mama Pearl and explained how I lost my food.

She wouldn't have me crying. "Now, boy com on in dis house. Dim no-good boys, I'm subject to tell dar mamas."

She made me sit on the sun porch and she fixed me a hot meal and made everything right. And she reminded me as I was finishing lunch that good little boys didn't fight, because vengeance belonged to God. Great, I thought, but God never showed up at school to help me out.

I spent almost a year sitting at my wooden desk in the one-room schoolhouse where Miss Maxey taught all eight grades. Next door we could see the new brick colored school under construction, and the men digging away the mounds of dirt for the cesspool.

Toward the end of the spring, the entire colored community looked forward to the eighth grade graduation exercises. For the colored students in Glen Allan, completing the eighth grade was equal to earning a high school diploma. Many of these students came from tenant-farmer and sharecropper families for whom having a son or daughter graduate the eighth grade was a major accomplishment. In some instances, colored kids who lived on farms had to board in Glen Allan to avail themselves of that educational opportunity.

One such boarder I'll always remember was Bernice, my cousin from the colony, who came to Glen Allan to live with "Tee" and complete the eighth grade. Tee (short for Auntie) was the town supplier of eggs and butter and milk, with quite a reputation for being a business lady. Bernice had been raised by Cousin Lulu Harris, a well-known church worker and landowner in the colored colony. Cousin Lulu believed in an education, and no expense was too great or sacrifice too difficult to keep her from giving Bernice the best. There was no school in the colony and no buses were running, so she rented a room from Tee so Bernice could pursue her schooling.

Bernice did complete the eighth grade and this gave her the opportunity to participate in the one great social/cultural event, the prom. On prom night each year, the eighth grade colored girls were our debutantes. This spring during the 1950s, Bernice would graduate and Cousin Lulu would sacrifice and buy her the floor-length taffeta-and-fishnet gown which the occasion required.

I must have gone to Tee's house to buy fresh buttermilk for Mama. Mama always bought fresh milk, butter and eggs from Tee. Even though Tee and Uncle Perry lived in town, their property was big enough to fence in an area for their cows and chickens. While I was at Tee's, Cousin Lulu Harris came into town with Bernice's gown. Long gowns weren't seen every day, and this dress was beautiful. Tee raved about it and Bernice just beamed as she pranced in front of the mirror with the new gown held up to her. I stood on the sidelines and watched as these two older colored women shared the excitement with Bernice and helped her get ready for her big night.

Everybody in Glen Allan knew when it was prom night and everybody would be watching, sitting on their front porches so they could see the young ladies and gentlemen walk by, perhaps hear the comments and compliments of the neighbors. I joined Ma Ponk on the front porch, the garret as she called it, and waited to see the start of the prom. It was easy for us to see because her house was just north of the colored school grounds. The school grounds were immaculate, and all the teachers would be present wearing the gowns and suits that had served them well at their colored college alma maters.

"There she is, there's Bernice."

I saw Bernice as the girls and their dates began to arrive. The girls arranged themselves on one side of the lawn with their gowns spread out as they gently knelt on the grass. The boys in their suits, and awkward to these once-every-year social graces, stood on the opposite side. With the deep green grass as their backdrop, with their gowns spread out in full circles around them, the girls looked like a living bouquet of colored flowers, waiting to be picked by the anxious boys. As a girl's name was called, a boy would walk over, hold out his hand, and she would stand to full height while he pinned a corsage on her dress. Together they would walk into the school where the colored band would be playing the blues. As I would later learn, they spent the best part of the night dancing — "slow dragging," as it was called. For those few hours, the eighth-grade prom transformed our colored community of sharecroppers and hired hands into a society of gentlemen and debutantes.

It was years before it would be my time to attend the prom, and in the meantime I watched as our first colored brick school was built. The new Glen Allan colored school was the result of the separate-but-equal policies. Many lives had passed through the one-room schoolhouse. Now a long concrete walk to the new school from the little wood-frame white building was our only link to a vanishing past.

I spent my first year in the new school awed by the tall ceiling and our first indoor toilets. Going to the toilet was a grand affair. With our teacher leading, we all lined up and waited our turn to use the urinals. We were not familiar with the handles that would let water into the long steel bowl. Each day we were told how to use the toilets and to keep in mind that they were not outhouses. It took awhile, but we eventually remembered to flush.

The Glen Allan colored school taught us more than how to flush toilets. It was our social life. As a young colored boy, I would learn about teenage romance at the colored school, for it was here we younger children surreptitiously watched the likes of Essie Short and Mack Chaney falling in love. Mack Chaney was my mother's younger brother and was known as the good-looking colored boy. He was considered a "good catch." Essie Short was one of the many daughters of Lillie Short, who lived on Linden Plantation. Even though the principal, Mr. Moore, and his teachers tried to keep young romance under control at the school, they were no match for the wiles of Essie and Mack, as they found any excuse to be together. The corner of the schoolhouse was their favorite place, and they probably never knew that all of us younger boys would sneak around behind the cafeteria and watch them steal kisses while they were hoping not to be caught by Miss Maxey.

The school also provided a forum for Miss Ross to indoctrinate us into the world of 4-H and teach us the importance of not saying ain't. And it did more. This red brick schoolhouse that had eight separate rooms was a focal point of pride for the colored community, the vehicle that would make our lives better. Even though we were being educated by colored teachers who in many instances came from backgrounds as deprived as our own, we were always motivated to be the best colored people. Our teachers made sure we knew the life histories of Dr. George Washington Carver, Mary McLeod Bethune, Marion Anderson and Jackie Robinson. We were encouraged to learn and to write about their lives. Over and over again, as we progressed through grades one through eight, these four great colored Americans were the subjects of countless essays. I would be out of college before I would fully realize that these four people, though they were great trailblazers, by no means represented the sum total of colored achievements.

By the time I reached the eighth grade, I knew the lives of the big four by memory. I had learned that chocolate milk did not come from colored cows, and most importantly, I had learned the value of flushing the commode. I knew Columbus discovered America and that Mr. Stennis and Mr. Eastland represented the state of Mississippi in the Congress of the United States. I knew little or nothing about my African heritage or of the great contributions made to American history by many notable coloreds. But I knew not to say ain't and I knew I wanted to be somebody; I was now ready to graduate.

In 1959, when I graduated from the eighth-grade, mine was among the last classes to follow the tradition of the eighth grade baccalaureate and commencement, which still entailed the traditional prom carried out in cotillion style. Our class was also among the last to feel the need to invite sympathetic white leaders to observe our rite of passage from unlearned field hands to young people with potential and purpose. As I sat among the 1959 eighth-grade graduates, I quietly listened to the principal, Mr. Moore, when he introduced my own Poppa, Elder Young. Poppa quietly charged us not to cause trouble, to be diligent in our work and to go as far as we could.

With the graduation over and the summer following close behind, I would prepare for my usual season of chopping cotton, but with great anticipation of the fall school year. I would be going to O'Bannon, a high school in Greenville. So excited was I to be going to a city school that I hardly took notice of the fact that the white high school of Glen Allan was only blocks from my house, and that I would have to travel more than 100 miles round trip each day to the colored high school in Greenville.

Miss Ross, Miss Maxey, and the other colored teachers had convinced us that no obstacle should stand in the way of our goals. Remember the lives of Carver, Bethune, Anderson and Robinson!

AUG 67

Chapter Three

Colored People,
Just Passing Time

Most of the colored people in Glen Allan, Mississippi, spent their lives working hard and never quite reaching their goals. But year after year, in spite of past failures when crops were bad and end-of-season bills amounted to more than the people made, they persisted. Working as maids seven days a week or sharecropping, picking cotton by day in the fall and chopping cotton by day during the summer, was their way of life. There was a strong work ethic when I was growing up in the South. Every colored person worked from the time he was old enough to drag a sack through the cotton fields. The work was back breaking, exhausting and sometimes degrading. It often required a mother to leave home in the morning to go prepare breakfast for a white family before her own children were fed. Everybody worked, because in spite of everything, most of the older people still clung fast to the belief that if you worked hard, you would get a slice of the American dream.

Never having been given much medical attention, their bodies showed signs of wear early, and their youthful agility quickly gave way to the aches and pains of age. Even though the people's time was orchestrated by the demands of the cotton fields, however, there were those precious rare occasions when they would get together just to pass the time.

Ma Ponk always worked hard, as did the others, only allowing herself to rest half days on Saturday, all day on Sunday and during those seasons between planting and harvesting cotton. Even though her feet gave her tremendous pain and her back ached more with each passing year, she never gave in to her ailments. She continued to pick and chop cotton. On Saturday mornings, however, she allowed herself the time to pursue one of her favorite pastimes, fishing on Lake Washington. Yet even her fishing was approached with zeal.

On those Saturdays, reluctantly, I'd join her and her three friends. To them, fishing was not only a chance to supplement ther food supply, it was a social event and an opportunity to gossip. Ma Ponk, Miss Doll, Miss Henrietta and Cousin Beauty formed the foursome that walked from the back of Glen Allan, past the uptown, to Lake Washington, where they staked out the best fishing spots. Most of the time they caught buckets of fish, but if by chance their luck ran foul, it would never be their fault. They blamed it on the water being too hot or cold, or they said the fish had gone downstream or upstream — whichever was more convenient.

I recall the day — after years of failure — that I caught my first and only three fish. I really didn't want to go fishing that day, but I didn't have much choice. I never wanted to go fishing, but Ma Ponk would not leave me at home alone. I trailed behind the four ladies, trying to pretend I wasn't with them, but close enough for Ma Ponk to feel comfortable that I wouldn't get into trouble. I knew that if I lagged too far behind, Ma Ponk's yells for me to catch up would clearly align me with them. Early on, I had carried my own pole, but for some reason, my catgut string always tangled beyond repair and Ma Ponk tired of untangling my line. The other ladies were convinced that I tangled the line on purpose.

I disliked the idea of gathering the worms even more than I disliked fishing. Ma Ponk insisted on growing her own worms behind the rundown chicken house. Reluctantly, I would dig for those long slimy baits, as we called them, and put them, along with moist soil, into a quart fruit jar. I dug them from the dark, damp side of the chicken coop, which never saw much sun and stayed wet from the dripping water. Each morning after our traditional breakfast of hoecakes, sausage and hot coffee, I would religiously take the coffee grounds and spread them beside the chicken coop. Ma Ponk believed the grounds added to the fertility of the bait habitat. The wet soil, along with constant exposure to used coffee grounds, must have worked. The baits were plentiful, long and fat, and according to Ma Ponk, just right — enough to cover the hook, with plenty left to dangle in the water.

On Saturday morning, I prepared the bucket, the fruit jar of baits, and got the poles down from the side of the house. Meanwhile, Ma Ponk was busy getting dressed in her fishing gear, making sure she had an ample supply of Garrett snuff. From Ma Ponk's house to the lake would normally be a short distance, but we had to make three additional stops, which lengthened the trip.

We stopped by Miss Doll's house first. She was almost ready, but she had to finish getting Mr. Jim's breakfast. He sat on their front porch dressed in khaki pants, black suspenders and a white T-shirt, fanning away the heat. Mr. Jim was one of those almost-white colored men whose skin would burn from the intense southern sun, so he always fanned the heat away. According to Ma Ponk, Miss Doll waited on him hand and foot. "Doll, ain't you 'bout ready?" Ma Ponk called back into her kitchen.

"Now, Ponk, you know Jim can't git 'round good. Lemme put a little peach jelly on his biscuit, pour his coffee and git his food to him."

"Jim, you ought to be shame of yourself, git up and help yourself, man."

Ma Ponk laughed as Miss Doll set up the little table on the porch for Mr. Jim. I watched as Miss Doll made sure her husband was settled and had all the food he needed. In the meantime, Ma Ponk had gathered our fishing poles, the bait jar and the water bucket. Together, we stood by Miss Doll's front gate, anxiously waiting for her to get her gear. Assured that Mr. Jim had plenty of food, Miss Doll, who was dressed except for her hat, went around to the back of their house and got her poles.

"Jim, leave dim dishes right dar on the table. I'll take care o' dim when I git back."

Mr. Jim , who was busy eating with one hand and fanning with the other, nodded as the three of us closed the big gate and headed uptown to pick up Miss Henrietta and Cousin Beauty.

Miss Doll and Ma Ponk walked ahead of me, catching up on the latest gossip. As usual, I walked slowly behind, wishing I could have stayed home or could be left at Cousin Savannah's to play with her grandson Bobby. Ma Ponk would always stop off at Savannah's for a few minutes to talk, but on fishing days, she would never let me stay and play. Ma Ponk would also stop and chat with her sister-in-law, Miss Callie, who lived next door to Savannah, and inquire about Callie's husband, Mr. Perry, after which we continued our slow walk.

By the time we got to Miss Florence's store, we could see Miss Henrietta and Cousin Beauty standing alongside the road with poles in hand, dressed and ready to go.

Like Miss Doll and Ma Ponk, they had their heads covered with wide straw hats, wore long-sleeved shirts and their everyday dresses. The four ladies with arm loads of fishing gear took up most of the narrow road, as they passed the post office to find their favorite fishing spots. Each one had a lucky spot. They were close enough to each other to continue talking, but far enough apart to keep their lines from tangling.

I sat on the bank of the lake with my feet dangling in the water as the four ladies joked, laughed, and spit snuff. Miss

Doll kept them laughing about Mr. Jim and his helplessness, while Miss Henrietta talked on and on about Mr. Will and all the people that came over to get a haircut without their two bits. Ma Ponk laughed and joked with them, but she wasn't one to give out much information. And Cousin Beauty was there to fish. She volunteered a bit of news about what happened Friday night at James Gatson's Café.

I was too young to visit James' café after dark, but even then I knew it was the right spot to be. All the northern cousins would include James' place on their itinerary during visits to Glen Allan. His jukebox and the food he served were in a class by themselves. James was a big man, dark complected, with a flashing smile, and he had a pretty young wife named Luella. Though located in the heart of the colored section in a small southern town, his café had an interior decor that allowed it not to be classified as a juke joint.

Cousin Beauty was a short-order cook at James' place on Friday and Saturday nights and had the reputation for being his best cook, but today she was concentrating her energies on catching catfish. I was getting more tired and bored by the minute. It seemed as if I had fished all my life, but I had never caught one fish.

Ma Ponk always kept me close to her so she could let me know when I had a bite. Ma Ponk's eyes were sharp and she watched both lines with great accuracy. I am glad she was watching that day, because otherwise I would have missed my fish.

"Boy, watch what ya doin'! You got a bite!" Ma Ponk yelled.

With lightning-quick action, she grabbed my poles, and together we pulled in my first white perch.

I was amazed. With one fish under my belt, I paid more attention to fishing. And much to everybody's surprise, I caught two more fish, more than I had ever caught in my life. It was a good Saturday morning.

Most of the time, the fish that were caught were cooked for dinner or for supper. Occasionally, however, the fish became part of a fun-filled and festive Sunday afternoon. During those rare get-togethers, Ma Ponk would turn her house and yard into a park, and she and her friends would start early in the afternoon to get the fire hot. They would get the big black iron skillets red-hot and the grease would pop all over the place. There would be loaves and loaves of Wonder bread and the number-three tubs would be filled with cold Pabst Blue Ribbon and Jax beer. Ma Ponk's long front porch was turned into a stage where the local musicians would come to play and sing the blues, and her small front yard was soon filled with colored people. They came from the colored colony, from Peru Plantation, from Wildwood, Grace, Valewood and the back of Greenfield. They walked, they rode in the backs of pickup trucks, they hitchhiked, and they came from down the road. Field hands, maids, schoolteachers, church deacons, and even the old folk — they were all there. Some were dressed in their Sunday best, while others wore their work clothes. Lost in the atmosphere of fun and frivolity, they joked, they laughed, they hugged and kissed each other as they ate fried fish, drank beer and lost themselves in the blues.

I was too little to really appreciate those wonderful musicians, but I remember their faces, and I can still hear their voices ringing out the blues as the then unknown Muddy

Waters (who came from a nearby plantation) tuned his guitar and loaned his deep soulful voice to their melodies of hurt, cheating love and those "you done me wrong" tunes. Long-legged ladies and strong-backed colored men moved gracefully as they melted their voices together.

They sang the blues with the excitement of a Sunday church service, and they all seemed lost in the soulful sound of the guitars. They knew it would be Monday in the morning, but this was their time, their Sunday, and they let the blues express the life they lived.

The smell of hot fish and the sound of the blues had faded. Ma Ponk's front porch was quiet now, except for the faint sound of hummingbirds going from flower to flower. And as the summertime and the fishing season passed, Ma Ponk and her friends would find new ways to spend their rare leisure time. With the fishing season over, the cotton not quite ready to pick, Ma Ponk would spend her days sorting boxes and boxes of quilting pieces, mending her broken-down fence, picking pecans and helping the neighbors kill hogs for the winter's meals. We would always kill hogs on Saturday so the complete day could be devoted to the killing, cutting, cooking and curing of the meat. The day we shot and killed our old sow was no different.

Ma Ponk had gotten me up early, and even though it wasn't cold, I had to dress warmly. Like Ma Pearl before her, Ma Ponk's favorite subject seemed to be the importance of keeping out the chill. After eating a quick breakfast, my cousins and I gathered by the hog pen so we could see the first people arrive. As I watched the old sow wallowing in her mud puddle, I recalled how I had helped to build the pen and had dug her water hole.

Even though we had built her a safe, secure pen, she would always find a way to root and get into the neighbors' mustard-green patch. Our neighbor, Aunt Mary Ann, upon discovering her garden torn apart, would immediately give us an accusing holler. By the time she got through pointing her fingers, you'd think we had purposely led the old sow into her garden. Then we'd have to get help to capture the old sow. Surrounded by people, all shouting and with large sticks in their hands, she'd grunt, squeal, and reluctantly go back into the pen.

Even though she had given us many sleepless nights by rooting out of her pen, I was still somewhat sad when the second shot was fired and the last grunt heard.

When it was all over and the old sow was dead, my cousins and I watched as Moses, my mother's husband, and the other men, caught the sow by the hind legs and placed her big red hairy body over the large barrel of hot boiling water. The body was dipped again and again into the water, until the hair became soft enough to be scraped away from the skin that would eventually become cracklings. I watched as the men laid the now hairless hog on a large board and began the task of cutting. Even when they weren't Ma Ponk's hogs being killed, she somehow seemed to be in charge. She moved about, giving orders while getting the iron pot ready to make lard. Ma Ponk assisted the men in correctly cutting up the hog, making sure none of the scores of people present walked away with the good parts.

Nearly every part of the hog was used, down to the hooves. A small portion of the odds and ends would be shared, but most was kept for the family.

Hams and shoulders were hung from the sides of the house to be cured, while two or three iron pots of water were set to boiling for making crackling skins, pork lard, and cleaning out the insides for chitterlings. When the day was almost over and most of the people had gone home, I stayed around. I wanted to see my grandfather Julius cooking fresh pork liver over an open fire.

He would fry at least half the liver, and he was known for seasoning and cooking it just right. Dressed in overalls and wearing an old felt hat with decades of sweat soaked around the band, with his pipe and match stick in his mouth, he would hum and quietly sing as he poked the fire and watched the iron skillet get red-hot.

The lard made a stinging sound as it hit the bottom of the skillet. Then Daddy Julius would take a handful of freshly cut liver, carefully roll it in flour, salt and pepper, and drop it into the waiting hot grease. He poked the fire and turned the liver, and all the while, we would be bathing in the aroma. When it turned deliciously brown on one side, he quickly turned it over, and soon the fall air would be filled with the wonderful smell of hot fried liver.

With the cooking and eating of the liver, hog-killing day ended. Now it was time to turn to other things.

Ma Ponk turned her mind to quilting. While the fall days were still fairly nice, she and her friends would sit on the front porch and piece together their intricate designs which would later become family heirlooms. Ma Ponk kept the quilting frame in the loft and I usually assisted in getting it down. We would clear out the front room and hang the frame in the center, securely anchored at all four sides. With the frame in place, the ladies would attach the lining, add the matted cotton and finally place their intricately designed top over the lining and cotton.

To do this, they'd come early in the morning and stay all day. Ma Ponk and her friends, while turning multicolored scraps into treasured designs learned from their mothers and grandmothers, would laugh, talk, discuss their children and their northern relatives. Their calloused hands swiftly and expertly sewed their feelings of love into the fabric they had salvaged and saved. Many of these handmade quilts would later be boxed and sent north as gifts and warm reminders of family left behind.

After the quilts were finished, Ma Ponk would wrap them in old newspapers and tie the boxes with cord. Then, on Saturday morning we'd take them to the post office to mail them north. On the way uptown, we'd stop by Miss Florence's store to rest and catch up on the news.

Miss Florence was from New Orleans. They said she was a Creole, but we never really knew. She and Mr. Isaiah had the only colored grocery store in Glen Allan at the time, and the only colored store that extended credit on the strength of your word. When we were between harvesting seasons, the store was a favorite hangout for the colored men. The store itself was not very large, a rather plain shotgun building built off the ground. It was shaded by an overgrown chinaberry tree that also provided shade and comfort for the men who met there daily to chew tobacco and discuss baseball. The ground under the tree was completely bald from the many chairs and soda crates that provided seating for the old men.

The inside of Miss Florence's store was very dark, and if it had not been for my love of doughnuts, I probably would not have visited many times. Nearly every time I went inside, I would see the same group of old men sitting at the far end by the meat box. These men, with bloodshot eyes framed by weatherworn colored skin, would be playing dominoes, not talking much, but concentrating on their strategic moves.

People came in and out of the store, but the old men were so preoccupied they never let shopping interrupt their leisure. And right there in their midst would be Miss Florence's husband, making his moves with the guys. Occasionally, I'd hear sounds of disagreement from one or two of the men, but never any physical movement. They never moved for customers; we worked our way around them, careful not to butt up against them or step on the old gray cat that also had ownership in the store.

Ma Ponk, Miss Florence and Miss Lottie Jones, the colored midwife, would talk for awhile. Ma Ponk always made it a point to talk with Miss Lottie because she was among the upper-class coloreds. She delivered just about all the colored babies, and she was known for strict recovery instructions — the new mother was not to take a bath, and her room was to be made completely dark, with no hint of sunshine coming in. I was too busy eating my doughnut to remember much of Ma Ponk's conversation with Miss Lottie. After filling in Ma Ponk and Miss Doll on the latest births, Miss Lottie excused herself, and the two of us proceeded uptown to ensure that the quilts made it north before the winter set in.

With the quilting done, the fences mended and baseball season over, both the men and women spent much of their time listening to boxing, the sport that brought the "brown bomber" Joe Louis into our homes. His name inspired pride; his fights would be relived for weeks and his victories celebrated forever. The "brown bomber" was our hero.

So few were the colored heroes that the ones we knew by name such as Joe Louis were like the neighbors who lived next door or down the road — a good ol' boy from the plantation that had gone north and made us proud. Joe Louis fights were subjects of sermons and sizzle for those Saturday-night conversations.

I don't remember the exact year, but I recall the night our front yard was filled with people who had come over to Ma Ponk's to listen to the fight. It was an important fight and everyone wanted to hear the "win" for themselves. There weren't very many radios in the colored section, but Ma Ponk had an old battery-operated one. It was important to her. She played it only on Sundays and for special occasions, and this was a special occasion.

A crowd of people started gathering early, bringing their Jax beer with them. Ma Ponk placed the radio in the window and unlatched the screen. She would never let that many people in her house, but her front porch was filled to capacity and there were grown men sitting on the ground as close to the bedroom window as possible.

With their bottles of beer and laughter, these didn't appear to be tired field hands. Their hard day's work wasn't slowing them down — not on this night. Their hero would be fighting tonight, and Joe Louis with his fists, quickness and punching power could say for them what they could never say for themselves. It was a sin to miss a Joe Louis fight. They all knew the exact time for the bell to ring, and Ma Ponk knew the exact time to turn on the radio. She didn't want to run the batteries down, which meant most of the prefight announcements were missed.

At eight o'clock someone mildly said, "It's time, Miss Ponk." She hooked the antenna wire into the screen and turned the knob. With a small amount of static, the fight was on. As the crowd listened, ignoring the bites of mosquitoes and night bugs, Joe Louis defended his title.

I remember the men jumping up and down, shadowboxing with each other. They gave step-by-step instructions, as if they were coaches and Joe Louis could hear each word. As they yelled and jumped, Ma Ponk would occasionally throw out her warning, "Don't step on my flowers, or I'll turn this darn thing off." Of course she never did, but for awhile, they were quieted — until a victory punch for Joe was announced.

The radio fight would go on into the night, too late for a little boy like me to hear it to the finish. I'd fall asleep on my cot by the window, while the colored people of Glen Allan successfully coached their hero to another victory.

Chapter Four

Luggage, Legs and Gorgeous Colored Women

The word spread through the cotton fields faster than a hoard of boll weevils through a gin filled with new cotton — the colored minstrel show was coming to Glen Allan. It's been more than thirty years ago, but I can remember it now as clearly as if it happened yesterday. Every pole that held electric wires was now a long, black, oil-soaked billboard announcing the yearly minstrel show.

It was all the excitement that any young male could handle. Minstrel shows brought the prettiest colored women from all over to our little entertainment-deprived town. Even though there would be a small fair to entertain the family, we all knew from past experience that the real fun would be at ten on Friday and Saturday nights when the big-top tent would hold a nearly all-male audience. Every boy in Glen Allan, white or colored, would try to figure out a way to sneak into the show.

The minstrel show and the town fair always took place on the fairgrounds. The fairgrounds were really just an irregularly shaped tract of land bordered on the east by the colored Mason's building (the only two-story building in the colored part of town) and on the west by the large Jewish grocery store. Only a paved road on the south separated the grounds from the quarters, a row of shotgun houses owned by a colored businessman named Mr. Walter. Later I would learn that the quarters had been used to incarcerate Japanese detainees during World War II. I never quite figured out who Mr. Walter purchased them from. Nevertheless, the quarters would play an important role in my maturity, because my aunt's best friend, Miss Bessie Glover, lived there. Ma Ponk always visited Miss Bessie and would let me visit by myself. Visiting the quarters and sitting on Miss Bessie's front step were as close as I could get to uptown, where all the action took place. Miss Bessie's steps provided me with a clear view of any activity on the fairgrounds.

Segregation had one advantage to my cousin Bobby and me. There were no hotel or motel accommodations to house the colored show girls, and we hoped to offer his house and my aunt's house as hotel rooms. In order to do this, we needed to make ourselves visible. What better place for visibility than the front steps of Miss Bessie's shotgun house. As soon as the posters appeared, we made it a point to be on Miss Bessie's porch overlooking the fairgrounds. We had to make sure one or two of the show girls stayed in our neighborhood.

It was on a Wednesday afternoon when we saw the first big trailer truck pull into town. We knew the beautiful girls with the long legs, shiny stockings and faces made up during the week would be close behind. As the big trucks pulled onto the fairgrounds, we could hardly sit still. Bobby was shorter than I was, but we both strained our necks and stood on our toes. Our toe standing finally paid off. We saw a shiny black car pull up and a white man got out, stretched and looked around. He then leaned into the car window and said something to the other occupants. And within seconds, all we saw were colored legs in shiny silk stockings piling out. The white man went around to the back of the car, opened the trunk and began taking out suitcase after suitcase and box after box.

Luggage, legs and gorgeous colored women were all Bobby and I needed to see. Without getting permission, we hit the streets running toward the long shiny black car.

"Boy, come here," the white man called.

"Yes, sir," rolled out of my mouth as easily as spit. In those days it seemed as if "Yes, sir" and white men went together hand in glove.

The tall skinny white man rattled coins in his pocket and said, "Do you know of someplace where we can rent a few rooms for these colored girls?"

"Yes, sir!" Bobby and I answered at the same time. We asked them to wait there and we'd go see how many rooms we could find. We both knew not to stop at the quarters because each shotgun house only had two rooms. Our best bet was to check with Cousin Beauty, Miss Florence, and Ma Ponk. We ran through the main street of Glen Allan, past the vacant lot behind Mr. Freid's house and straight to Cousin Beauty's. When Cousin Beauty was not cooking sweet potato pies, she was fishing. Boy, how we hoped and prayed that she'd be cooking that day!

"Miss Beauty, Miss Beauty!" we called as we barged through her front door. "It's us, Cliff and Bobby."

Cousin Beauty was a formidable sight as she came hurrying from the kitchen, a buxom colored woman whose dark skin had gained her the name "Black Beauty." No one knew her age, but she was totally wrinkle free with a Coke-bottle figure. While wiping her hands on her apron, she asked the reason for our loud calling. When we explained that the minstrel show was looking for rooms, she must have smelled money. She took off her apron, went back to the kitchen and within moments she was locking her front door and heading uptown to the fairgrounds.

Bobby and I kept running toward the back part of the colored section; we had two more stops to make.

On the way to Ma Ponk's house, we stopped by Miss Florence's store. She too was excited as we inquired about rooms. She got Mr. Isaiah to watch the store while she turned all her dignified weight toward uptown. With only a few blocks left, we ran down to Ma Ponk's house. Ma Ponk was sitting on the front porch talking to Miss Doll. Without breaking our stride, we butted right into the middle of their conversation.

"Ma Ponk, the white man at the fairgrounds wants to know if you can rent out two beds to the show girls till the minstrel show is over."

Ma Ponk must have smelled money also. "I sho can," she said. Without a good apology, she excused herself from Miss Doll, gathered her glasses and spit cup, and went quickly into her house to get her hat.

Bobby and I raced back to the fairgrounds. We did not see anyone immediately, and our hearts sank. Then we heard laughter from around the side of the big truck. We peeked around the truck just in time to see the white men putting a top on a liquor bottle. We didn't know their names, so I just blurted out, "We back."

By the time we explained about the rooms we'd gotten, all three new hotel owners were there, Ma Ponk, Miss Florence, and Cousin Beauty. I never knew the room rate, but the white guy with his generous heart pitched us a dollar apiece. A dollar! A whole dollar, not a nickel or a quarter, but a dollar — and it all belonged to me! We quickly shoved the money into our pockets and began to walk behind the entourage of ladies headed to the colored section.

Friday night didn't come quickly enough, but it finally came. Before the fun could start, I had to bathe. I hated getting ready for those weekly baths, but Ma Ponk insisted. And getting a bath required much preparation. There was no hot water to be had simply by turning a faucet handle. Preparation began with the gathering of firewood for the wood stove. Once the stove was hot, Ma Ponk put water into the iron kettle. After what seemed like hours, the kettle would be whistling and Ma Ponk would call me, "Boy, git that tub in here and brang your clean underwear wit you."

"Yes'm", I answered, as I ran out the back door to get the number-three galvanized tub. As always, I placed the tub in the middle of the kitchen floor and watched as Ma Ponk poured in the kettle of hot water, to which she added cold water from the water bucket. It took at least three buckets of cold water to cool the kettle of hot water and make enough water to sit in.

With no more hot water on tap, I had to act quickly to get my bath. Ma Ponk had hung quilts at the windows, so I could undress now. I was excited; I was getting a chance to go to the fair. The water was just right. I slipped into the tub and began soaping down. As I washed my face I closed my eyes, and all I could see were visions of gorgeous colored ladies with rouge on their cheeks.

After dressing in the steam-filled kitchen, I dragged the tub to the back porch, tipped it over and watched the soapy water run through the cracks and form a puddle under the house. Smelling like soap and Mum deodorant and my hair pasted with Gloversmain grease, I was ready.

Just about everybody I knew was at the fair. There were white people and colored people having fun together, but being careful not to speak or fraternize. Everyone was drunk on the smells of the fair, of cotton candy and commercially made popcorn. In spite of all the fun in the booths, Bobby and I could hardly wait 'til they announced the adult show.

It was going to be hard to sneak in. Except for the entrance, all the sides around the tent were securely staked. As we wandered aimlessly through the crowds, we could feel the excitement mounting. The crowd got bigger and bigger around the entrance to the tent. Of course we were too young to be allowed in and we didn't have any money. The green-back dollar bill the white man had given each of us had long since been spent at Miss Florence's store. Just when we thought we were out of luck, one of the colored show girls who stayed at Cousin Beauty's house beckoned for us to help carry her makeup case and bags of shoes into the tent.

We walked closely behind the tall beautiful lady with colors on her face such as we had never seen in Glen Allan. As she walked through the rows of seats, men were whistling and calling out phrases that weren't meant for our ears. The more they whistled, the slower she walked.

We placed her bags by the dressing-room entrance and waited for a minute or two. As we were about to leave, she said, "Wait, boys." She gave us twenty-five cents apiece and told us to leave. We left the dressing-room area quickly, but instead of exiting when we got to the last row, we jumped down behind a stack of boxes.

Finally it was show time — the music started. Men jumped to their feet shouting. The few women in the audience covered their eyes and giggled. There on stage in living color were about ten of the most beautiful colored girls we had ever seen. As the music played, they began to dance and move. Bobby and I watched wide-eyed, and with the crowd, we were transported to a different world — a world of sensual beauty that we probably should not have seen, but will always remember.

Those same colored ladies we'd seen earlier were now all dressed up in shining pants and had large multicolored feathers growing out of their hair. They were beautiful! And as they danced and moved about the stage, the mostly white male audience went wild. Before my innocent eyes, one of the men ran toward the stage, was subdued by guards and held to the ground. While he was being held down, one of the pretty ladies came close to the edge of the stage, leaned over and beckoned for him to come on the stage. He tried to move, but the guards held him firmly. Bobby tried to whisper in my ear, but I just brushed him away. I was too scared to talk — afraid of what I was seeing.

The colored dancer finally jumped up from the stage, laughed out loud and went back to dancing with the others. The music played faster and the crowd cheered louder. The dancers would bump and grind their way to the edge of the stage, then they would all laugh together, whirl, and dance back. As the music blared and the dancers moved, the curtains opened, and out came colored men wearing tuxedos and smoking long cigars. They started talking back and forth with each other and with the dancers. The more they talked and joked, the louder the roar of the crowd. And as the two men came closer downstage, my eyes widened. They were white men with their faces painted black!

The minstrel show ended after Saturday night's performance. And as in years before, everybody complained about being cheated. Miss Florence, Cousin Beauty and Ma Ponk had all made a few extra dollars, however, and the men of the town would talk for months about the dancers. Bobby and I didn't feel cheated! We looked forward to next year.

With the departure of the minstrel show the fairgrounds were empty except for debris. Only holes in the ground remained where the big tent had been. The city-style entertainment had left, and we were left with the Dixie Theater, the town's only movie house. The Dixie wasn't much to look at even back then, but it was uptown, it was white brick and it did have big four-color posters advertising the movies. There was only one entrance for the white and the colored, but once having paid for the ticket, we would enter the show using opposite sides of a heavy curtain. The coloreds used the left side, the whites used the right side. We all eased into the darkness hoping not to bump into each other as we found our seats in one of the two sections racially separated by a small aisle down the middle of the theater.

Ma Ponk didn't really approve of moviegoing, but reluctantly, on occasion, she would take me as far as the quarters where Miss Bessie Ann lived. From there she could stand on the porch and make sure I did not go across the street to Mr. Walter's café, which was the established colored juke joint. Mr. Walter's café was the only colored business uptown on the main street of Glen Allan, and it was right across from the Dixie Theater. Allowing me to go to the movies was a major concession, but never would Ma Ponk knowingly let me go near a juke joint.

On a Saturday evening during the late summer or early fall, Ma Ponk would get in her visiting with her friend in the quarters, thereby giving me the rare opportunity to go to the Dixie. I recall the Saturday they were showing the last episode of the *Green Archer,* a serial. I wanted to go badly, but fifty cents was not easy to come by. After begging Ma Ponk and getting no response, I decided to walk the road and kick rocks. My Grandfather Julius saw me crying and inquired into the matter. Sensing opportunity, I poured out my heart to him. Soon after, my tear-soaked hands were clutching fifty cents.

I ran home to Ma Ponk. "Can I go to the show?" I begged. "Daddy Julius just gave me fifty cents."

Finally she agreed to a visit with Miss Bessie Ann and I knew that meant "yes." Miss Bessie Ann and her husband Mr. Cape Glover were very hospitable, and always glad to have Ma Ponk visit. Their little front porch with a wooden swing on one end and two chairs on the opposite was just big enough to seat them and one guest. I usually sat on the steps. But tonight, I would be going to the Dixie.

Most of the time Ma Ponk would let me walk over to the Dixie alone, but tonight she and Miss Bessie decided they would walk with me to ensure that nobody bothered me and that I went straight into the picture show. I walked just slightly ahead of them, while they gossiped and talked. We finally reached the Dixie, but there were too many whites milling around the door, so Ma Ponk made me wait with her off to the side until the whites had all entered. Finally, I walked up and paid my fifty cents. I almost went in on the wrong side of the curtain, but the white cashier called me back.

"Boy, don't you know your side?"

"Yes, sir," I replied as I quickly moved to the left.

It was dark inside the show, but in a few moments my eyes adjusted and I walked up near the front, where I finally saw my two uncles, Eugene and Hurley. They were in their teens and they really weren't all that thrilled with a kid like me sitting with them. They were afraid I'd tell on them if they started messing around with girls or trying to smoke a Lucky Strike. They let me sit by them, but I could tell they didn't particularly care for it. I tried to act big as I watched the *Green Archer* on the movie screen. Then they offered me a cigarette. I hadn't ever smoked, but tonight looked like as good a time as any to try it. There I sat surrounded by darkness and grinning relatives. They all were smoking; I had to try. I reluctantly accepted the Lucky Strike that had passed through at least five mouths.

"Don't inhale."

"Blow the smoke out."

"Hold your head back."

I tried to do everything they told me, all at once. I choked; my eyes filled with tears; I began coughing and couldn't stop. It was awful. They laughed and laughed. I was humiliated, but glad to be alive. Smoking was NOT fun, but at least now they could rest easy, knowing I wouldn't tell. Finally they left me alone and I settled back to watch the *Green Archer.*

After the movie, I swore to them that I'd never tell, and then I ran as fast as I could to the quarters.

"Boy, what's wrong?" Ma Ponk asked when she saw me. "Did them peckerwoods bother you?"

I assured her no one had bothered me, and that I just wanted to get home. We sat on the front porch for a few minutes more, but finally we made our move to leave. I would sleep well tonight. The Green Archer had not died and I had attempted my first and last cigarette.

As a boy I never went to a real big movie house like the ones in Greenville, the Queen City of the Delta. I relied primarily on the yearly minstrel shows and those infrequent trips to the Dixie Theater. My heroes were Buster Crabbe, Johnny Mack Brown and the Green Archer. If not for Mr. Moore, the principal of the colored elementary school, I guess I would have grown up not knowing about the likes of the bandleader Louis Jordan and the singer Ethel Waters. Once every month, Mr. Moore would rent and show a colored movie as a school fund raiser. The colored movies were never shown at the Dixie. They featured an all-black cast and, unlike the standard serials and westerns, their intended audience was colored. I would always go to the colored movie, and Ma Ponk never objected, because we lived directly across from the school and it wasn't uptown like the Dixie.

The movies were always musicals with limited plots. The music was the colored big-band sound and the singers were the best. The world of the colored stars was completely unreal to me. Even though I saw them talking, singing and joking their way across the screen, their dress and style were far removed from the life I knew. And since most of the colored movies were made around the same few stars, they became known in name and characterization. We looked forward to seeing them and escaping into their world. We all were convinced this was reality, just north of the Mason-Dixon line.

GENESIS

CHAPTER 1

the beginning God created the
ven and the earth.

And the earth was without form,
void; and darkness *was* upon the
e of the deep. And the Spirit of God
ved upon the face of the waters.

And God said, Let there be light:
d there was light.

And God saw the light, that *it was*
od: and God divided the light from
e darkness.

5 And God called the light Day, and
the darkness he called Night. And the
evening and the morning were the first
ay.

6 ¶And God said, Let there be a firmament in the midst of the waters, and
et it divide the waters from the waters.

7 And God made the firmament, and
divided the waters which *were* under
the firmament from the waters which
were above the firmament: and it was
so.

8 And God called the firmament
Heaven. And the evening and the morning were the second day.

9 ¶And God said, Let the waters under the heaven be gathered together
unto one place, and let the dry *land* appear: and it was so.

10 And God called the dry *land* Earth;
and the gathering together of the
waters called he Seas: and God saw
that *it was* good.

11 And God said, Let the earth bring
forth grass, the herb yielding seed, *and*
the fruit tree yielding fruit after his
kind, whose seed *is* in itself, upon the
earth: and it was so.

12 And the earth brought forth grass,
and herb yielding seed after his kind,
and the tree yielding fruit, whose seed
was in itself, after his kind: and God
saw that *it was* good.

13 And the evening and the morning
were the third day.

14 ¶And God said, Let there be lights
in the firmament of the heaven to divide the day from the night; and let
them be for signs, and for seasons, and
for days, and years:

15 And let them be for lights in the
firmament of the heaven to give light
upon the earth: and it was so.

16 And God made two great lights;
... light to rule the day, and ... made

17 And God set them in the firmament of the heaven to give light upon
the earth,

18 And to rule over the day and over
the night, and to divide the light from
the darkness: and God saw that *it was*
good.

19 And the evening and the morning
were the fourth day.

20 ¶And God said, Let the waters
bring forth abundantly the moving
creature that hath life, and fowl *that*
may fly above the earth in the open firmament of heaven.

21 And God created great whales,
and every living creature that moveth,
which the waters brought forth abundantly, after their kind, and every
winged fowl after his kind: and God
saw that *it was* good.

22 And God blessed them, saying, Be
fruitful, and multiply, and fill the waters
in the seas, and let fowl multiply in
the earth.

23 And the evening and the morning
were the fifth day.

24 ¶And God said, Let the earth bring
forth the living creature after his kind,
cattle, and creeping thing, and beast of
the earth after his kind: and it was so.

25 And God made the beast of the
earth after his kind, and cattle after
their kind, and every thing that creepeth upon the earth after his kind: and
God saw that *it was* good.

26 ¶And God said, Let us make man
in our image, after our likeness: and let
them have dominion over the fish of
the sea, and over the fowl of the air, and
over the cattle, and over all the earth,
and over every creeping thing that
creepeth upon the earth.

27 So God created man in his *own*
image, in the image of God created he
him; male and female created he them.

28 And God blessed them, and God
said unto them, Be fruitful, and multiply, and replenish the earth, and sub-
due it: and have dominion over the
fish of the sea, and over the fowl of the
air, and over every living thing that
moveth upon the earth.

29 ¶And God said, Behold, I have giv-
en you every herb bearing seed, which
is upon the face of all the earth, and
every tree, in the which *is* the fruit of a
tree yielding seed; to you it shall be for
meat.

30 And to every beast of the earth,
and to every fowl of the air, and to

Chapter Five

SCHOOL DAYS 1952-53
GLEN ALLEN

Fear, and Hope:
Childhood Memories

"I don't want to go!" I cried, as my aunt ordered me to the store for a pound of Maxwell House coffee, the drip kind. I didn't want to explain to her why, but I didn't want to go.

It was a Sunday morning and I knew there was only one store open. The white couple who ran this store had a reputation for keeping us coloreds in our place, and their one son, an unhapppy acne-covered adolescent, followed in their footsteps, taking out his frustrations on little colored kids. At thirteen, I was skinny. My voice had not yet changed and I had not yet developed "field" muscles. I dreaded going into that store. My fear was real; my knees would shake and my voice would quiver each time I was forced to make this Sunday morning trip.

The son was called Billy Roy — in my hometown, white guys always had two names. When Ma Ponk mentioned his parents' store, I'd see Billy Roy — blackheads, T-shirt, penny loafers and all — right in the middle of my mind, daring me to breathe. There he would be, slouched on their counter top, chewing gum and drinking an R.C. Cola.

One pound of Maxwell House was seventy cents and my aunt had given me a dollar bill. There was a penny tax and I was to spend the extra four pennies and bring twenty-five cents home. It was not a hard task, but I would much rather have gone to the Chinese store than face Billy Roy on a Sunday morning.

The supermarket concept had not yet reached us. We had to ask the storekeeper for whatever we needed when we went grocery shopping in Glen Allan. When I got to the store and walked in, all my fears became reality. There, waiting like an acne-faced white god, was Billy Roy.

"What you want, boy?" snapped Billy Roy as he combed his hair. "Make it quick, I ain't got all day." Nervous as I was, I quickly walked over to the counter and pointed in the general direction of Maxwell House coffee. I thought I asked for drip, but maybe I didn't. Anyway, he gave me a can of coffee and dropped it in a bag with my change. He didn't smile at all, just stood there being stone-cold cool.

I ran home as fast as I could and gave my aunt the bag and her change. Just as I was leaving, my aunt yelled, "Boy, git back in this house! I told you drip and this ain't drip. You take this right back and exchange it."

Stone-cold Billy Roy was still drinking his big RC when I got back to the store. As mildly as a thirteen-year-old could I said, "You gave me the wrong coffee." Billy Roy's acne got bigger and blood rushed to his already red face. "Boy, cain't you read? Why didn't you ask for the right kind in the beginning?" he yelled.

After enduring his angry tirade I finally got my drip coffee. I had good reason to be afraid of Billy Roy. Most of us lived on the edge in this era of segregation, in this society created so that even a sixteen-year-old white kid could take advantage of a position of power. Billy Roy represented much of what I came to despise. There were, however, moments when the difference in color did not make such a deep wedge in Glen Allan. Such a time was the day Miss Shugg's house burned down.

I guess it was nearly three in the afternoon when I first heard the cry of "fire!" Sure enough, the blue sky was gradually changing to amber, and white clouds were turning gray and black. There was a fire on the south end of Glen Allan, just below the colored school.

By the time I ran across the school ground and through Aunt Mary Foster's yard, I could see the blaze and feel the heat. Shugg Payne's house was on fire.

Miss Shugg was a colored lady who lived directly across the street from a white family, the Brittons. Miss Shugg was known for her devout religious practices and for her love of dogs. The lady's house was infested with dogs. When the fire broke out, Miss Shugg could not be stopped from running back into the house to save her puppies.

Everybody in town, black and white, gathered in the street in front of Shugg's house as the flames engulfed the little wood structure. In those days, there were no fire engines in Glen Allan, just arms and buckets. Quickly, a bucket line formed to fight the blaze, and suddenly I noticed something I'd never seen before in Glen Allan. The racial separation which was ordinarily so strictly observed seemed to disappear in this moment of emergency. The bucket line was integrated. White and colored men and women stood shoulder to shoulder, passing buckets of water from the pump in the Brittons' yard hand to hand all the way across the street to Miss Shugg's. Black and white people were risking their lives together as they filed in and out of the burning house, saving what they could. Even after the blaze got too hot and the smoke too dense to allow people in the house, the bucket line kept the water coming, until it became obvious that their gallant effort would be no match for the consuming flames.

The fire that had pulled Glen Allan together finally burned out. With just ashes left, the crowd parted speaking words of sorrow and the blacks and whites went their separate ways.

As for Miss Shugg, she survived the fire. It was rumored that she had a good deal of money stuck securely between the pages of her Bible, but when her house caught fire, all she thought about was her dogs. In all those trips back inside to round them up, she never thought to get the Bible. She managed to save every one of the puppies, but the Bible went up in smoke, along with all Miss Shugg's money.

Chapter Six

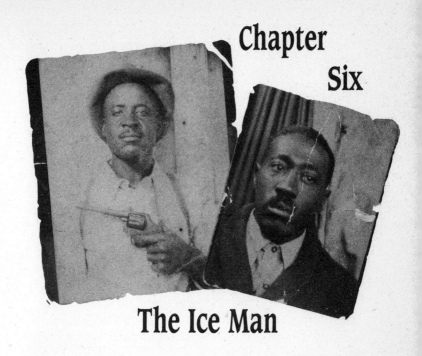

The Ice Man

Surely if my Uncle Cleve were alive today, he'd find a reason to be a black Republican. He was short, neatly dressed and conservative. Uncle Cleve came from Coldwater, Mississippi. I know very little about his early life with my Great-aunt Willie, but I do recall his strong personality and the impact he had on my life growing up in Glen Allan.

I never heard him raise his voice. When he talked, he always talked politics and demonstrated a real business sense. Independence and nonconversance were his most notable characteristics. I called him Uncle Cleve, Ma Ponk called him Bro. Cleve and every other colored person called him Mr. Cleve. The white community with which he had contact called him Mormon, his last name, their badge of respect.

Uncle Cleve, Mr. Cleve, Bro. Cleve or Mormon — he was my first employer. From him, I learned a sense of responsibility that undergirds my approach today. He ran the only icehouse in town. Refrigerators were a rarity in the colored community and among the poor whites, and nearly all the small businesses used ice to keep their goods from spoiling. Only Mr. Cleve provided the ice needed in Glen Allan. Twice daily, we'd see him driving the red flatbed truck up and down the streets, announcing "The iceman is here." For years, I would run alongside the truck as Uncle Cleve stopped at each house and chipped his sales of fifteen or thirty pounds of ice. Occasionally someone would buy fifty pounds, but that was rare. He was always quick, responsive and very polite — not given to extra conversation when waiting on his customer. His business made our lives better, and he was always received as a welcome sight.

Being an assistant to Mr. Cleve was viewed as a good job, and I couldn't wait until I was old enough to work with my cousin Joe, Uncle Cleve's son. Uncle Cleve had been training me by taking me with him to Hollandale, Mississippi, to buy ice from the ice factory. We would ride to Hollandale together, just the two of us. I recall the trip taking hours, but really it was very short. We'd drive down the road eating salami and crackers and every once in while he would talk to me about life.

"Yes, git you a good pattern and follow it. Always be early for work, and save fifty cents out of every dollar you make."

I didn't try to answer. I just sat in the cab of the truck and listened as he continued talking. All I wanted was the chance to show him that I could handle the big three-hundred-pound blocks of ice. If I could prove my ability to handle the big blocks, he would let me work at his icehouse.

Finally one Saturday, he gave me the chance. I must have been about twelve years old. Child-labor laws weren't in vogue in Glen Allan, and when you were strong enough to handle the job, nobody worried about how old you were. I could hardly sleep the Friday night before, although Ma Ponk had no problem getting me into bed on my little cot by the front windows.

"Boy, git to bed early, 'cause Bro. Cleve will leave you if you ain't ready to go when he comes by," Ma Ponk told me as she securely tucked me in bed.

Saturday morning didn't come soon enough. I found myself waking up nearly every hour, straining my eyes to see the hands on the clock. Finally I heard Ma Ponk's voice through the quilts. "Cliff, git up and git some food in you, 'cause you know Bro. Cleve ain't gonna stop."

No sooner had she spoken than I jumped from bed and ran to get the wash pan so I could wash up before eating my breakfast. The smell of hot oil sausages and grits floated through the house, and I could hardly wait. How lucky could I be — a trip to Hollandale with Uncle Cleve, *and* my favorite breakfast. The food went fast and I found myself ready and waiting when Uncle Cleve came by. True to form, he was a little early.

"Bye, Ma Ponk!" I yelled as I jumped from the porch to the ground.

Our trip was not unusual, but this time I would have the chance to show my uncle that I was big enough to help him with the business.

"Cleve, pull your truck in next" a colored man yelled as we pulled up to the Hollandale Icehouse.

Uncle Cleve let me out of the cab and told me to take the steps to the dock; he'd meet me there. He never made suggestions. You simply did what he told you, and quickly. After parking the truck so the bed would be against the dock, Uncle Cleve came around to the side where I was standing.

"Okay, Cliff, we'll see if you can handle the big one."

As we walked into the icehouse, all I could see was a cold vapor rising from hundreds of blocks of ice. Each block weighed three hundred pounds. Standing inside the door, I felt the chill as Uncle Cleve took the giant ice hook off the wall.

"Cliff, pay attention." Uncle Cleve proceeded to show me how to put the ice hook securely into the block, while using my knee as an anchor.

I watched and I watched and I watched. Finally, it was my turn. I walked over to a huge block of ice and carefully repeated what I had been shown many times. I securely hooked my ice, carefully placed my knee and began to gently pull the block to the floor. Before I could get fearful, I had finished. The three-hundred-pound block of ice was on the floor, and I was pulling it out to the trucks.

"New helper you got, Mormon?" one of the white men asked.

"Yes, sir," Uncle Cleve nodded as he watched me load the truck for the very first time.

My ride home could not have been sweeter. Uncle Cleve stopped by a local store and bought me a large grape soda and a moon pie — my reward. We didn't say much on the way back, but we both knew it had been a good day.

Many months later, nearing the end of the summer, Uncle Cleve promised to take me with him to Jackson as a gift for having done a good job for him. The day of our trip finally arrived. It started out as one of the happiest days of my life. My uncle was taking me to Jackson to the biggest tent show that had ever come our way. Ma Ponk got me all dressed up in my Sunday church clothes, combed my hair until my scalp was sore and had me ready at least two hours early. Uncle Cleve was a slow driver so we were going to leave in plenty of time to get to the seven o'clock grand opening.

I was ready at three o'clock and sitting out on the front steps waiting for the familiar sound of Uncle's 1947 green International truck that purred like a kitten. Ma Ponk and I were waiting, and there was absolutely no way of missing Uncle Cleve. When the truck pulled up, I almost jumped out of my pants, but Uncle Cleve only smiled slightly as I ran around to the passenger's side and tucked myself firmly in, secure with the knowledge that tonight was going to be a really big night for me. Uncle Cleve was very confident, only telling me that he never messed with the small-town minstrel shows that came to Glen Allan to rob you blind. If he was going to waste his time and spend his money, it would be at something like the big show that we were going to in Jackson.

I know I counted every tree and rock between Glen Allan and Jackson, because Uncle drove so slowly. He never hurried about anything. Moving meticulously, like a well-greased snail, he'd get the work of two men done in half the time. His driving was the same, perfect execution of the rules, never speeding, just fast enough to beat running.

It was almost 150 miles to Jackson. Ma Ponk didn't even pack me a lunch, because Uncle Cleve had promised to buy my lunch. Packed lunches in greasy brown paper bags were for old church ladies, not the two of us.

Finally we reached Jackson. There were more bright lights than I had ever seen. This was a large city, not like Glen Allan. Uncle Cleve took the city in stride. After all, he had been to Memphis, and Jackson was just another city to him. To me, however, Jackson was the biggest and the brightest. It even had uniformed policemen directing the traffic, and I saw my first traffic jam.

I was so excited about being in a city I didn't realize we had gotten near the show grounds. There seemed to be hundreds of cars and people. But my uncle knew where we were going. He parked the truck and held my hand tightly as we followed the crowd. Finally we got to the main gate, where a big curly-headed white man reached down and took our tickets. We were ushered in with the crowds of other people to a tent that seemed big enough to cover the whole world.

White people were everywhere, laughing and talking and eating popcorn and pulling their children behind them, as we all headed toward the big tent.

It was so crowded in the tent and we were so far back that I could hardly see, but I remember when those gigantic curtains opened and I saw all those beautiful ladies in sequined stockings. I could hardly sit still. I know I was too small to fully appreciate that beauty, but the glitter I understood. The music was loud all around us and sweaty men were yelling and whistling but my uncle just smiled slightly, ate one piece of popcorn at a time, and watched.

We couldn't have been there any more than twenty minutes when the usher came over to us and said, "I am sorry, but this ain't the night for niggers."

My uncle's smile dropped from his face and his warm eyes became cold as steel as he jerked me up and we walked out. We hadn't even seen half the show.

The long trip back was completely silent. I sat in the car, miserable, trying not to cry. I was too young to understand why this had happened to us, and my uncle would not explain.

Chapter Seven

Colored Politics in a Small Southern Town

The 1988 presidential race was interesting, and as a black American, I found myself very much emotionally involved. For many of us, there was only one presidential candidate, Jesse Jackson, the black preacher. His outspokenness, his campaign and his media visibility were jolts to my memory. When I was growing up in the colored section of Glen Allan, political activism was virtually nonexistent — a hushed and maybe secret tryst into the white world at best. I remember only one overtly threatening act on the part of the whites in our community, when they burned Hodding Carter in effigy in the white town park because he had advocated racial equality in his Greenville newspaper.

There were, however, quieter incidents. I remember one such incident on a hog killing day at the old house by the colored school. Ma Ponk and I had come over early to start the fire under the big iron pot. Today, she would be teaching my mother how to make pork chitterlings. All my uncles and a few cousins were there also. While the adults made ready to slaughter the two hogs, my cousins and I were playing cowboys and Indians on the unfinished porch that was to be a room someday. These cool fall mornings were good for playing cowboys and Indians, our favorite game.

With all the adults involved in slaughtering the hogs, we children were left virtually alone to go into the storage shed and create whatever world we could imagine. I loved going into the shed on the end of the back porch. It was filled with surprises. There was an old water-stained box that had been on the top shelf of the shed for many years. Today I was curious about what was in it, and we pulled it down and opened it. Inside was an American flag, with forty-eight stars. It was so big we could hardly spread it out. The bright colors of the flag, the red, white and blue, seemed such a contrast to the drab unpainted room. We completely unfolded it over the bare floor boards. We were so involved in making the flag part of our fun that we didn't notice the adults had stopped talking.

"Don't let that flag tetch the ground!" my grandfather yelled suddenly, as he moved from the backyard to the side of the house where we were playing. "Boy, don't you know if white folks see you messing with this here flag like this, they subject to kill you?"

Stunned, we didn't answer. We just dropped the flag and ran over to the school ground. My Grandpa Julius must have folded it up and put it back into the water-stained box, but I never touched it again. I couldn't understand why we had a white person's flag at the old house, but it was never mentioned again.

Politics were seldom discussed in our colored world. The only thing that was openly talked about was the inequity of the poll-tax system which kept so many colored people from voting. Those who lived on plantations were told whom to vote for, or encouraged not to vote. For the most part, we were a disenfranchised people, and only a brave few of us managed to exercise our voting rights.

I remember one fall day when my parents, my sister Claudette and I were all crowded into the cab of the family's old red pickup. I remember we were out for a visit, because on Saturdays we often went to Peru Plantation to see our cousins. As we drove by the white park and past the colored Masons' hall, we headed uptown on the street that passed the Dixie Theater and Mr. Jake Stein's grocery store. Suddenly, I noticed something I'd never seen before, a huge picture of a white man that covered the whole side of the store. It was a political billboard advertising the presidential candidate Adlai Stevenson. I leaned my head out of the truck and asked my mother, "Who is that picture?" I recall her abrupt response.

"Boy, don't let no white folk hear you say nothing about that man. That's white folks' business. We ain't got nothing to do with it."

Within moments, our truck had passed the store, and I can't remember whether we went home or to visit, but I do know I never asked that question again. My world was colored, and at that point, politics were seldom discussed.

The red truck brings to mind another incident, because it was that truck which kept my mother and her husband off welfare. In Glen Allan, welfare was not looked on as something a good colored person still young enough to work wanted to be involved in, but there was a time when my family was so desperately poor my mother went to apply for welfare. When she got there, however, she learned that to get welfare, she and her husband would have to sell the red truck, their only means of transportation. They didn't sell the truck, and we didn't get welfare, so we never became part of the system.

I remember the first time political action really entered our colored world. We never went to church on Thursday nights, but for some reason, on this Thursday we were getting ready to go. Miss Doll had told Ma Ponk about a special meeting to be held at Saint Mark's Missionary Baptist Church. Even though she was tired, Ma Ponk rushed to get ready, then she bundled me up and got her last dip of snuff. As we walked past Aunt May Ann's house, Ma Ponk called out.

"May Ann, let's go, gal. You so slow!"

Aunt May Ann was known for going to all special meetings, but Ma Ponk called her uppity because she spent so much time dressing up — even on weekdays.

"Ponk, I'm coming. Let me put on a little rouge."

At last Aunt May Ann came out to meet us.

"May Ann, do you thank I should take this boy?" Ma Ponk whispered. "I hear it could be dangerous. Rumor is we might be watched."

"Oh, it's all right."

"I hope so, but I know those peckerwoods don't like this one bit."

Saint Mark's, the family's church, was not far. Ma Ponk and Aunt May Ann talked softly and secretively as we walked. We could see the church but not the usual activity of members standing outside laughing and talking. The white frame building with the pointed bell tower just stood there in the darkness waiting for us.

I didn't hear any singing, but when we walked in, the church was packed. There was no preacher in the pulpit and I had not heard about a revival, so I knew this was an unusual meeting. Colored faces glanced nervously at each other while watching the doors and windows. There were deacons standing at the front and back of the church, and when they were sure everyone was in, the doors were barred.

Preacher Hurn was old, with a hump in his back, but he got up and walked to the front of the church. In a low voice he began to sing a favorite Dr. Watts hymn:

"Father, I stretch my hands to thee. No other help I know. If thou withdraw thyself from me, where other shall I go?"

I watched as he stood under the single hanging light bulb, his balding head shining and moving with the slow beat of the song. The rest of the church joined in softly. After his song was over, he slowly walked back to his seat, while another deacon got up from his chair and walked to the front of the church. He bowed on one knee in front of the wooden altar and began to lead the prayer:

"This evening, my heavenly father, I come to thee, knee bent and body already bowed. I ask you to stretch your hands of mercy out and protect our brother as he starts his walk through the valley of the shadow of death. . . ."

As he continued his prayer, a fervor swept through the church. People began to cry, and the women began to moan through their tears, "Have mercy, Lawd!" I recall seeing men in church that night that I had not seen on Sundays. They too were moved during the prayer and began to mutter under their breath, "It's been too long, Lawd."

As the prayer ended, a stillness came over the crowd, and one of the leading colored men of our town, Deacon Joe Maxey, stood and moved quickly to the front. Tonight he was well dressed. He was unusually somber, and with a trace of tears in his eyes, he began to pace back and forth.

"I'm leaving tonight for Baltimore. Ya'll know where I'm going and what I'm going to do. I need your prayers. Don't fear for me. God has gone before me and the Devil can't do me no harm."

Deacon Maxey was a known speech maker, but tonight his talk was short. As he finished speaking, an offering was raised. The deacons blessed the money and presented it to him, after which they prayed over him. When the prayer was over, we all quietly left. While Ma Ponk, Aunt May Ann and I slowly walked home along the gravel road, I'd hear Ma Ponk say under her breath, "Keep 'im, Lawd."

Later I would learn that Deacon Maxey had gone to an NAACP national meeting to voice our concerns for equal rights, a subject not openly discussed in a small southern town.

Chapter Eight

Some Glad Morning,
Some Glad Day,
I'll Fly Away

It was closer to our hearts than our homes — the colored church. It was more than an institution, it was the very heartbeat of our lives. Our church was all our own, beyond the influence of whites, with its own societal structure.

Even when colored people moved north, they took with them their church structure. The Baptist church, of which my family was a part, had (and has) a big network under the auspices of the National Baptist Convention. A small colored Baptist church in Glen Allan, Mississippi, and a large colored Baptist church in Saint Louis, Missouri, had the same moderator, used the same Sunday-school books, and went to the same conferences. And whether north or south, large or small, the colored church was a totally black experience.

Ma Ponk made sure I was regularly immersed in the colored-church world. As early as I remember, I spent my Sundays, both night and day, attending church with Ma Ponk. No matter the hard workweek, we all looked forward to Sunday when we would dress in our best and meet our friends.

Sunday morning came in easy and Ma Ponk would let me sleep late. The smell of hotcakes and homemade pork sausages fried in lard would float through the house. Ma Ponk only had to call once.

When I got to the kitchen Ma Ponk would be moving around the black iron stove in her starched white dress. She was on the Mothers' Board of the church, and as a church mother, she was required to wear white to Sunday services. Ma Ponk made sure her dress was hand starched and washed in rainwater to ensure that extra whiteness. She was careful not to get any spots on her dress as she skillfully turned the hotcakes and brewed her Maxwell House drip coffee.

"Don't git in my way. Now, you jes' sit down on the back porch and eat your food. We got to leave for church pretty soon," Ma Ponk said.

She began to pin up her hair. She had extra long silky black hair, but she felt it was unchristian to wear it down, so she would plait her hair into long braids and wrap those braids around her head. Finally to ensure her hairpins held safely, she would wrap her head in a white scarf.

In white shoes, silk stockings, starched white dress and her white scarf, Ma Ponk was ready for church. Ma Ponk's parents and grandparents were founding members of Saint Mark's Missionary Baptist Church and she was considered one of the leaders. It was the fourth Sunday, Pastoral Day, and our little colored neighborhood was all abuzz as the gravel roads were filled with people dressed in their best, laughing and joking on the way to the sanctuary, our church.

Pastoral Sunday was the one day a month when our official elected pastor would be there to deliver the message. Other Sundays, he would be at one of the other churches he served, and Saint Mark's would have to make do with a pinch hitter. It was no great honor to be asked to speak on those off Sundays, because everybody knew that the crowd would be small and the offering (from which preachers were paid) would be low. People who felt the call to preach and positioned themselves to fill in on off Sundays were called jackleg preachers, because they had no churches of their own.

Today, however, there would be no jackleg preacher. It was Pastoral Sunday, and there was a great feeling of togetherness as we neared the church. Women in their white dresses and black Sunday hats and men in their Sunday suits with their best brightly colored ties and shined shoes were shaking each other's hands, hugging and kissing the children as we took our turns climbing the steps into the main sanctuary.

Today, field hands were deacons, and maids were ushers, mothers of the church, or trustees. The church transformed the ordinary into an institution of social and economic significance. A hard week of field work forgotten, the maid's aprons laid to rest, and the tractors in the shed, these colored men and women had entered a world that was all their own. Rough hands softened with Royal Crown grease were positioned to praise. As a young boy, I sat quietly in my seat and waited for the services to start. The church was designed for us children to be seen and not heard, and if by chance we talked or got caught chewing gum, Miss Nola or one of the ever-present ushers would take a long control stick and crack us on the head. The church rules were strict, and the ushers made sure nothing interfered with the high spirit of the service.

While the ushers proceeded to order the crowd, three of the deacons would place their chairs in front of the altar, for they were charged with starting the service. As I watched the activity of the church, my eyes fell on Mother Luella Byrd. Mother Byrd was not only head of the Mothers' Board, but basically in charge of the church. There she sat, dressed in white with her black cape draped over her shoulders, her arms folded and her face set. Once Mother Byrd had taken her position, God could begin to move. Ma Ponk reluctantly paid homage to Mother Byrd, but under her breath she could be heard saying, "Byrd acts like she owns Saint Mark's."

And it was true; Mother Byrd was without question the matriarch of the church. Not only was she an influencing and stabilizing factor for Saint Mark's, but her demand for perfection and self-respect and her high hopes for the colored race will always be with me. She was slightly overweight and walked with her left foot turned outward. When she walked, her hands would be clasped behind her back, and whatever the day, she was dressed as if she were in charge.

Mother Byrd was known for her Easter program which was a must for all the children of the church. We were expected to know our parts to perfection. Securing a commitment from the parents, she would give us our speeches one month in advance and hold practices weekly. Our limited resources never bothered her, only spurred her on to pull out of us the best she knew to be there. For her, Saint Mark's Missionary Baptist Church was Washington Cathedral and we, her pupils, were the cream of the crop. With determination, she'd take our unorganized minds, lack of ambition, and bad grammar and create a top-quality program. Mother Byrd had no formal education herself, but she encouraged us to work hard and get an education. She was a proponent of black pride long before it became fashionable as she tuned out our excuses and channeled our efforts.

Every Sunday morning, Mother Byrd was seated front and center at Saint Mark's by the time the singing began. As the song "I'll Fly Away" rang throughout the building, she rocked back and forth while the congregation rocked from side to side . While they sang, Elder Thomas began to preach. The singing and the preaching would blend and build together to a fever pitch. Elder Thomas, like an athlete at peak performance, paced the front of the church and preached until he was covered with sweat and the entire congregation was caught up in the spiritual fervor.

By contrast with Sunday morning, Sunday night was rather dull in Glen Allan unless we were lucky enough to have a "singing" at one of the neighboring churches. Ma Ponk always went to the Sunday-night singing. She felt that one could never get enough of God. A good cowboy movie or a chance for me to play softball would not override her decision to go to a singing. Of course she knew the dates, places and times for each one, because announcements were tacked on every electrical pole in town and lying in every ditch.

Quartet singers represented more than colored harmonizing; they were examples of the good life. If those singers happened to have come from Memphis, our excitement could not be contained. You see, we knew that all the really good singers lived in Memphis. If the singers were coming from Memphis, Saint Mark's wasn't good enough for them. They would sing at Mount Zion Baptist Church. While most of the colored churches in our small town were wood shingled, Mount Zion was covered with white asbestos siding and had concrete steps leading into the main sanctuary.

I remember the Sunday after church at Saint Mark's when Ma Ponk and her friend Miss Doll decided we'd go to the big quartet singing at Mount Zion. Every colored person in Glen Allan wanted to be part of the Mount Zion singing. Ma Ponk didn't wear white because tonight she would not be on the mothers' bench. Tonight, she dressed in her best, a multi-colored jersey dress, and wore her black straw hat. I wore my one good outfit, my brown gabardines and a plaid shirt.

The Memphis singers, usually all men, were role models of sorts for the young colored males and objects of fantasy for the women. These singers were dressed in the latest northern fashions, and their hair was ironed to their heads. Their shiny straightened hair would glisten under the exposed sixty-watt bulbs. The women idolized them, and the young black males would come out in droves.

According to Ma Ponk, you couldn't get these people out for real church, but at a singing they'd take up good seats and the Christians would have to stand. There they'd be, the young male field hands dressed in gabardines and nylon puckered shirts. The more fortunate ones wore suits and pointed-toe shoes. For the women, this singing brought out more fishnet and taffeta material than any other event. Their hair would be tightly curled and pressed to their heads, held in place by rhinestone combs. The ladies — young and old — would come early to get a front seat so they could reach out and touch their perspiring idols and occasionally faint and very innocently fall into the arms of the lead singer.

And the singers would sing until their clothes were dripping with perspiration and their guitar strings were begging for mercy. Once the singing got going good, they'd rip off their ties and coats and throw them to the crowd. We were all enthralled by the Memphis sound. Even Ma Ponk, not known for unnecessary emotion, would rock back and forth while making sure her hands remained tightly folded. Mount Zion hosted all the Memphis singing stars of those years, even the late great Sam Cooke.

As the last encore ended and the applause became part of the night, we left Mount Zion with new conversation good for at least three working days. The week's field work would go easier now because the colored quartet had come to town.

We spent most of the summer working hard in the fields and relishing the interruptions brought by the church. As the summer came to its end, Ma Ponk, our family, our friends and our town began preparing for the social events that usually took place this time of year. High on the list of such social events was the Annual Sister-workers Day.

I had heard about the sister-workers all my life. Nearly everyone I knew was a member, and Cousin Lulu Harris from the colored colony was the treasurer of one of the larger "works." Ma Ponk paid her dues religiously and ensured that her family was doing the same. The sister-workers was an auxiliary to the colored church. Its primary purpose was to provide funds to families of its members on the deaths of loved ones. Even though it was organized, operated and staffed by women, membership was open to all. The monthly fee was less than a dollar per person, and at death, sixty dollars would be given to the deceased person's family. Ma Ponk belonged to five works as they were collectively called.

Once yearly, the local sister-workers would have their year-end conference, commonly called Annual Day. Annual Day centered around friends and baskets of individually pre-pared food. Even people who had moved north would arrange their yearly visits to coincide with this day. They would come back to Glen Allan to pay their annual assess-ment in person and, of course, visit their many friends and relatives. It was a much-needed and well-attended social event.

I have fond memories of the sweet-potato pies Cousin Beauty baked for the Annual Day, and of Cousin Savannah's famous pound cake. Although Ma Ponk was a member in good standing of several works and never missed an Annual Day, she and her older sister Aunt Lurlean were never known for their fancy cooking. Ma Ponk fixed a basket of food which consisted of plain store-bought cake and chicken fried by my mother, Mary. Aunt Lurlean, who was treasurer of the Saint Mark's work, prepared a basket of store-bought food. All Saturday morning everybody else in Glen Allan was cooking. The smells of cakes, pies and fried chicken mingled in the streets. Finding the right-sized cardboard boxes to make our baskets was my job. I'd make numerous trips to the Chinaman's store to get my arm load of boxes, big enough to hold all the food without the tops pressing down. I could hardly wait for 2:30 p.m. For eleven months, we had all looked forward to this day. The Annual Day meant the best food ever.

We'd get to church early, because Ma Ponk was responsible for making sure the aluminum water bucket was filled with water and ice and there were at least two drinking glasses. Of course Ma Ponk always brought her own glass. Under no circumstances would she drink from the community cup. After getting the bucket filled with cold water, we went around the church, opened all the windows and placed the funeral home fans in each seat. As we put out the paper fans, we could see people beginning to arrive.

All the neatly tied pasteboard boxes of food were placed in the communion room until it was time to serve: Sweet-potato pies, jelly cakes, chocolate cakes, fried chicken, baked rabbit, fried pork chops and pork-sausage sandwiches. I just prayed that Mother Byrd would not talk forever. Eventually, the last song was sung, the last prayer prayed, and I was ready to sample as much as Ma Ponk would let me.

Ma Ponk never ate while there, but she enjoyed the fellowship. Everybody else feasted and talked for hours until at last it was time to leave. We both laughed as we saw some people who had come with no boxes, leaving with full loads. As the Annual Day ended, Ma Ponk and I stayed behind to close the windows and lock the church. A soft wind came along to blow away the used paper napkins, and neighborhood dogs gathered to enjoy the scraps. Ma Ponk was tired, but her dues were paid for another year, and between the money from her works and her burial policy, she would not be ashamed to die.

Not only did the colored church prepare us for death financially, it made sure our souls were prepared as well, because every year Saint Mark's revival came on the heels of Annual Day. Ma Ponk, as one of the church's mothers, was intimately involved in the yearly revival.

It seemed as if God always waited until the end of the cotton-chopping season and right before the picking started to prompt the church to get the revival fires started. All the small colored churches around Glen Allan and neighboring plantations were getting ready for revival. The sinners had been notified. God was coming to town, and his front men were filled with holy indignation. They gave the sinners warning that this year's revival might be their last chance to miss hell's fury.

Handbills with misspelled words were passed out. Ma Ponk, Mother Byrd and all the soldiers of the church began to pick sinners for which they would especially pray. Seven days had been set aside for the Saint Mark's revival, starting on Monday and ending on Sunday with a public baptismal service at Lake Washington. Ma Ponk was happy that the Reverend Thomas would be preaching this year's revival, because he was her pastor whom she had elected. "Look out, Satan! God's man's entering your territory." Ma Ponk couldn't wait until the ending Sunday when the Rev. Thomas would march the candidates (the newly saved sinners) right down the main street of Glen Allan so the Devil could see them with his own eyes.

This would be a good year for souls, according to Ma Ponk and Cousin Lulu Harris. They had just finished having a big revival in the colored colony. Cousin Lulu always came to town to visit Ma Ponk and to keep her informed on the Lord's work. Ten souls were saved in the colony, then brought to Glen Allan to be baptized. But nothing would compare with the Reverend Thomas' revival. This would be the big one. This would be the one where I would get a chance to be saved.

It was Monday night. The revival had started. Saint Mark's was packed with people, all fanning themselves with paper funeral home fans in the hot one-room church. As the singing began, the deacons and mothers of Saint Mark's lifted their voices to the Lord, filling the rafters with song. Aunt Willie Mae, a good singer with a strong voice, was leading the congregation.

"I'll fly away. I'll fly away. Some glad morning, I'll fly away."

As they rocked and clapped, their spirits seemed to have soared to heights unknown. And in the midst of this fervent praise, the Reverend L. T. Thomas, an imposing colored preacher, rose from behind the altar and lifted his voice to start the revival. He had a voice as deep as a well and as clear as a noon bell. The Reverend Thomas' eyes seemed to focus directly on me, my cousin Bobby, and my Uncle Eugene.

"Can you fly away? Will you have a glad morning someday?" The Reverend Thomas bellowed over the singing. As the congregation sang more softly, the Reverend Thomas asked the deacons to set up the mourners' bench, a place designated in the front of the church for sinners to come, sit and be surrounded by praying church folk.

This was our year. We had been an embarrassment to our families too long. So without much coercion from the pulpit, the three of us led the way to the mourners' bench. As we took our seats and others joined us, there were shouts of acclamation, "Amen!" and "Praise God!" all over the church. Once seated up front, we were soon forgotten. The services went on at a high-fevered pitch while we, the town sinners, just sat and looked.

The mourners' bench was a world unto itself. While sitting on the bench, we would try to make each other laugh while the preaching and singing was going on around us. My cousin Bobby was chewing bubblegum. I was trying to concentrate on my lost soul when Bobby tapped me on the shoulder. Just as I turned to look a huge pink bubble burst all over his face. Nearing the end of the service, the Reverend Abe Brown, who was my great uncle and Bobby's great-grandfather, was asked to pray the salvation prayer for the mourners' bench. On request, we all fell to our knees. As we knelt there, Bobby reached over and pinched me, and before I could pinch him back I felt Uncle Abe's hot breath on my neck. He laid hands on me and Bobby and began to pray:

"Lord, look on these sinners. Look on my grandson Bobby and my nephew Cliff. They is good boys, but they don't know you. . . ."

As Uncle Abe prayed, we buried our heads in our hands and prayed not for our salvation, but rather that Uncle Abe would not pray all night. Finally, the services came to an end and we were instructed to find a quiet secluded place to pray during the day and to make sure we asked God to give us a sign of significance that our lives had been changed.

The week's revival was coming to an end; true to his reputation, the Reverend Thomas had cracked the ranks of Satan's army. More than one dozen people had come to the Lord. Both Bobby and Eugene were saved, but for some reason, in spite of my praying and finding my secluded spot, I did not get saved that year.

Even though I didn't confess religion, Ma Ponk and the whole church were overjoyed. Their prayers were answered. Their revival had saved more souls than the one in the colored colony. By now everyone knew who was saved and the colored section of Glen Allan was preparing for the big baptismal service.

The revival services ended on the Saturday night before the fourth Sunday. This would be the day to baptize. The Reverend Thomas had requested the deacons and the mothers and the candidates for baptism to meet at the church at least one hour prior to the time to march to Lake Washington. Ma Ponk, being one of the head mothers of the church, was among the ones requested. She would assist the female candidates in dressing. Today, Ma Ponk was all dressed in white from head to toe. This was a sacred responsibility; she had even left her snuff behind. My grandfather Julius was responsible for getting the men ready. Their goal was to create a visible difference between those new initiates of the Kingdom and the rest of the world. The candidates, both men and women, were dressed in long white gowns and their heads were covered with white caps. Except for the color of their skin, hair, and shoes, the baptismal party was an army of walking whiteness. With the Reverend Thomas leading the group, they marched from Saint Mark's church down the middle of the paved road and right through the uptown section of Glen Allan to the lake. With singing and clapping, crying and praising, the baptismal procession began. Everybody was arranged in order of importance, with the Reverend Thomas in the front of the parade and the deacons behind him. The candidates followed, with the mothers of the church walking religiously behind, their arms loaded with towels and sheets.

As they marched, they sang, "Take me to the Jordan, take me to the Jordan, I want to be baptized." In ones and twos, others of us joined in the march. By the time we were passing the local juke joints, we had begun singing, "Lord, wash me whiter than snow." While the Lord was washing us whiter than snow, we were preparing to walk through the residential part of town where Glen Allan's whites lived. When we got close to their homes, the Reverend Thomas would say, "Look to God, pay no attention to the peckerwoods. They don't respect nothin'." He talked, we marched, we sang and we looked straight ahead and paid no attention to the teenage white boys who looked on and laughed.

The crowds had grown, and when the procession reached the banks of the lake, there were scores of people sitting on their cars waiting to see the candidates go under the water and come up. At the lake, the singing slowed and we watched where we were walking, because the rumor had started that Deacon Roy had killed a rattlesnake while cutting a path down the hill to the bank so he could set the stakes out in the lake. The water was crystal clear and the air was filled with low humming sounds coming from the church members and visitors. Everybody was just waiting on the signal to burst out in the favorite baptismal song, "Wade in the Water, Children."

With his hands uplifted and flanked on either side by his deacons, the Reverend Thomas offered prayer and called for the first candidate. It was a man; the town drunk had come to Christ. He told about his troubles, the religious dreams he had experienced while on the mourners' bench, and those left standing on the banks began to cry and raise their hands in agreement with the candidate's testimony.

"On the banks of stormy Jordan I stand. . . ."

Lake Washington wasn't Jordan, but it served as a good substitute. When the baptism was over and the fervor had died down, when the soaked bodies were wrapped in the big towels, we all began to leave. Those of us who had marched through the city in triumph were now left to thumb a ride home. It was a good revival, even though I probably let Ma Ponk down by not getting saved. She just nodded and said, "Maybe next year."

Our lives centered around the colored church. It provided the framework for civic involvement, the backdrop for leadership, a safe place for social gatherings, where our babies were blessed, our families married and our dead respected. Yes, the colored church became the sanctuary for our dreams and the closet for our secrets, and even the funerals were representative of all we were, and what we hoped to become.

One of the funerals I remember was that of Miss Hester. When Miss Hester died, it was late at night, but somehow Granddaddy Julius knew, and the church bells tolled. Ma Ponk always heard the bells. She always listened for the midday crowing of the roosters, and during this particular week, the roosters had crowed continuously, so Ma Ponk knew someone would die, but she didn't know who it would be. As the bell tolled, she got up and looked out the window, trying to determine which house had lights on. It would be hard to sleep, not knowing who had passed away.

The next morning early, Ma Ponk went out to her backyard, talked across the fence to her neighbor, and found out Miss Hester had died. Miss Hester, like some others in our town, was a mulatto. She was nearly white. Her mother was colored and her father was a white farmer. She kept a big picture of her father on horseback hanging in her parlor. Oftentimes she and Ma Ponk, who was part Jewish, would spend hours arguing about the amount of blood required to make them totally white. Even though strict racial segregation was the order of the day, it somehow seemed to have slipped at night, because throughout our colored community were numerous men, women and children who were called "high yaller." Ma Ponk, herself being one, always said, "nearly ever' peckerwood got a nigger in his closet." Ma Ponk always liked to tell about the time the colored soldier came to town after the war to visit his white uncle who lived across the field from us.

According to her, he was received well and spent the day with them. After that, he left, went north and never returned.

Miss Hester's death brought up a flood of such conversations, because all her near-white sisters and brothers from around Jackson would be coming to the funeral. It would be a big funeral, held at Mount Zion Baptist Church, so Miss Doll, Ma Ponk and I went early to get good seats.

While waiting for the family processional to begin, I recall Ma Ponk and Miss Doll reminiscing about the time another high yaller lady had died. During that funeral, a well-dressed lady walked in. She had red hair, and her freckled face was partially veiled. As she walked up near the front, the ushers were confused. They didn't know if she was white or colored. Ma Ponk recalled that as the lady walked by she recognized her. It was her childhood friend Lizzie who had not been to Glen Allen for more than forty years. In those days, many high yaller colored choose to move north and live a white life.

Ma Ponk and Miss Doll probably would have unlocked every closet in town had it not been for the preacher asking the church to rise. The body was being brought in, with all of Miss Hester's nearly white relatives following close behind.

The choir began singing and the funeral directors busied themselves arranging the flowers on the casket. The choir led us in singing "Farther Along," then the mistress of ceremonies came to the front and began the program that would provide opportunity for Miss Hester's neighbors and church members to speak about her and pay their last respects. Finally, all the memories were shared, and it was time to hear the special singing. As she started the familiar melody of the bittersweet funeral hymn, the singer was singing not only for Miss Hester but for all under the sound of her voice:

> *"If when you give the best of your service,*
> *Telling the world*
> *That the Savior has come,*
> *Be not dismayed*
> *When men don't believe you.*
> *He'll understand and say 'well done.'"*

Chapter Nine

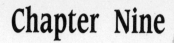

The End of a Season

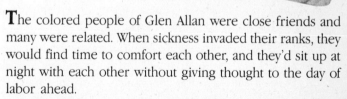

The colored people of Glen Allan were close friends and many were related. When sickness invaded their ranks, they would find time to comfort each other, and they'd sit up at night with each other without giving thought to the day of labor ahead.

During sickness, the women would sit for hours talking, sharing memories, recalling their past and the pasts of others. It was during these times that I learned much about our family, our history and where we had come from.

As I remember the illness of my great-grandmother, I recall her many friends and how they all came to sit with her. They came to comfort. They came to visit.

It was the end of the season and we had picked the last of the cotton. Only a few plantations had scraps left, and just about everybody in Glen Allan had put their sacks away for the year.

The leaves had fallen off the big pecan tree and all the chinaberries had been gathered for the fires used to smoke the winter's meat. Ma Ponk had not raised hogs this year, so we had no need to keep the chinaberries, but as always, we stocked up on the cut wood, logs and coal. For the last month, Ma Ponk had been spending her evenings and Saturdays taking care of my great-grandmother, Mama Pearl. This Saturday, however, Ma Ponk didn't go around to Mama Pearl and Poppa's house, the "big house," mainly because we had to get in the coal and wood. Usually Ma Ponk would be full of talk, trying to get me to work harder, but not this Saturday. In fact, she had not been herself for days. She was worried about Mama Pearl. Ma Ponk had said if Mama Pearl didn't get well before the winter, she doubted that she'd make it.

We worked fast, or at least Ma Ponk did. I was not yet six, too young to be of much help. We did little talking. Ma Ponk had me bundled up to keep out the chill but as she worked she seemed not to notice me. We finally finished moving the coal from the front yard into the coal house. After finishing, we went in and Ma Ponk warmed up some leftover chicken wings and rice. She fixed our plates and took them to the front bedroom. We would always eat there at dusk so we could look out the window and see all the comings and goings. After finishing our food, we sat in silence in a room lighted only by the flames from the wood stove. Ma Ponk sat in her rocking chair, rocking back and forth and looking through the limbs of the big pecan tree, straining to see Mama Pearl's roof. Occasionally she would hum her father's favorite hymn, "Precious Lord," as we both just sat in the darkness watching the night slowly come into our lives.

There was no rush to undress. We sat ready to go. Ma Ponk could be counted on to be there for Mama Pearl if she needed her tonight.

I curled up on the foot of the big iron bed and watched Ma Ponk. While lying down partially asleep, I saw her stand up and move quickly to the front door. She had seen her Cousin Beauty walking toward her house.

"Ponk, it's me, Beauty. Pearl ain't well at all. In fact, Elder Young wants us to sit up with her till Dr. Duke come."

"All right, Beauty," Ma Ponk said. "I just knew that Ma Pearl was gittin' no better."

"Lord, chile," said Ma Ponk, looking over at me on the bed, "I sho hate to git you out in this cold, but we better go."

While Cousin Beauty waited by the wooden gate, Ma Ponk got her heavy coat, a small can of Garrett snuff and her spit cup, blew out the lamp and made ready to leave.

With the darkness, the old pecan tree by the public water hydrant looked massive and scary. We walked as fast as we could, our silence interrupted only by the sound of the gravel under our feet and a whistling of wind through the pecan branches. As we passed Mr. Stanley's shotgun house, Mrs. Stanley called from her front door.

"Ponk, how is Miss Pearl? I hear she got worse about a hour ago. Ya'll call me if you need me. I'll be home."

I could see Mama Pearl's house as we got closer. The front steps were tall and wide. The house had been built after the flood of 1927, so the foundation was built off the ground. Ma Ponk went in first and we followed. The front room, nicely furnished with black leather couches and chairs, was filled with people just sitting and waiting. As we walked in, Ma Ponk's presence was acknowledged. I quietly listened, too young to really understand, as the other people explained the situation. I looked from face to face. No one was smiling. They talked and nodded their heads. I curled up in Poppa's big chair. I wanted to see Mama Pearl, but I didn't say anything. I felt alone in the crowded room. In Poppa's big chair, I could look into the small bedroom each time someone went in or came out. The small bedroom off the living room, Mama Pearl's and Poppa's bedroom, had always been my favorite place. It was cheery, and I loved sitting on the big brass bed with the soft mattress, where Mama Pearl would let me take my naps. Tonight, however, there was no laughter in that room, only silent sadness. The normally bright room was dim and the pretty spread was gone, with quilts in its stead. As the hour grew later, I watched the faces grow more solemn. My relatives and friends of Mama Pearl continued going in and out of the small bedroom.

"She won't last the night," Cousin Beauty said as she walked out.

Ma Ponk wasn't much for talking or passing opinions. She just sat by the wood stove and rocked. It was a cold night, but the big iron heater kept the front room cozy and warm.

Everyone sat in a semicircle around it, making sure there was a big spit can in the middle.

As they sat and talked, Ma Ponk came over and put a quilt over me where I lay curled up in Poppa's big chair. Occasionally someone would get up and check on Grandmother. The rest of the time, we all listened to Miss Sue, a ninety-year-old colored lady who remembered much about our families' lives. Miss Sue talked about General Wade Hampton coming into the delta to set up his plantation after the Civil War. She also recalled the arrival of my great-grandfather Sidney Peters in the delta with his half-Jewish wife, Miss Rose.

"Yeah, Ponk, I sho knowed your people. Course, I wuz just a girl, but I 'member when Sid and Rose Peters come up from the hills. Yor Pa had a fine carriage, pulled by a team of white horses. He was the blackest colored man I'd seen, and Miss Rose, well, we all thought she wuz white. Yes, Miss Rose's Jewish folk lived down by Mayerville."

Miss Sue probably would have continued to talk about Ma Ponk's grandparents, but Cousin Beauty interrupted her.

"Sue, what happened to Ole Man Josh Wade's boy?"

"Well, after his colored mama died, Mr. Josh sent him north. He never came back. Course you know, mostly all dem real high yallers went north and passed for white. Course, once you pass, you can't come back round again."

They must have talked for hours or listened as Miss Sue talked about the old folks, long since dead. As the conversation continued into the night, I dozed off. But when I awoke, I remember the flurry of activity. Ma Ponk was sitting on the side of the bed wiping Mama Pearl's head. I could see fully into the room now; the door was wide open. There was Mama

Pearl, not saying a word, just looking as if through the ceiling. I could hear sniffling, and bits of conversation.

"It's her heart."

"Pearl knew it all the time."

"She told me at church 'bout a week ago that she felt she was giving her last covenant."

"But Pearl's all right, she got good religion."

We could hear Ma Ponk talk as she wiped the perspiration. "Now Mama Pearl, you'll be all right. Hold on 'til Dr. Duke gets here."

Dr. Duke was white and the town's doctor. He took care of the coloreds and the white. And no matter the time, he would come. But before he got there I heard Mama Pearl cry out, "I'm leaving ya'll, the angels are coming to get me." Ma Ponk, through tears, said, "Don't say that. You'll be all right." But this time Mama Pearl couldn't be coaxed back to life. She was tired — her heart was tired. It was the end of her season.

Except for the sound of crying, the small room was still. Mama Pearl was loved by everybody, but she was gone. Just as the leaves had left the pecan trees and the blue sky turned gray, her life had passed into the night. But Ma Ponk was strong. She told everyone to meet her at the house in the morning, so the bedclothes could be washed and the house cleaned. After they left, Ma Ponk was silent as she went into the room, combed Mama Pearl's hair and straightened the bed.

We waited with Poppa for the funeral-home people. After a few hours of sad silence, they came, arranged for the wake and the funeral, and took Mama Pearl's body away. I watched as Poppa closed the door to the room. I saw his tears, and I knew tears meant sadness. Ma Ponk put on her coat, got her spit cup and we told Poppa good night. While we were leaving, Saint Mark's church bells began to toll. Another soldier was gone.

Chapter Ten

All In A Day's Work

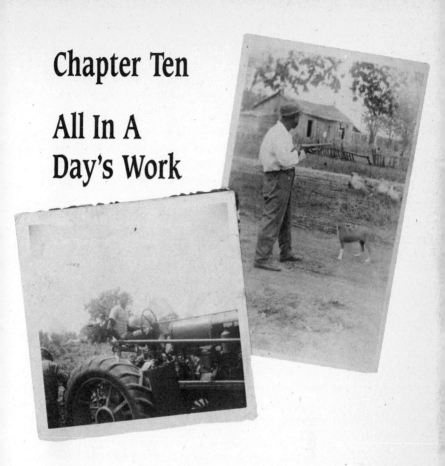

Everybody in Glen Allan, especially those of us who were colored, were getting ready for the "picking-cotton" season. All the field trucks had been repaired and most of the hired haulers had gone around to the various houses, making sure they had ample workers committed. And as usual, Ma Ponk and I had agreed to work with Mr. Walter.

The fields were almost ready to burst out in a sea of whiteness framed by the green leaves and stalks. We could tell because all the pink and white flowers had dropped off and the cotton bolls were bursting with life. And as the sun and the rain worked together, we could see spots of fluffy white cotton beginning to dot the acres and acres of fields. We could feel it in the air; the summer fun was almost over. Within weeks now, we'd all be getting up with the chickens and standing ready for the field truck.

And this year, I had promised myself I'd pick two hundred pounds. Picking two hundred pounds was the badge of harvest accomplishment. I had yet to make my family proud. I had gotten close, even past one hundred fifty pounds, but I hadn't quite been able to break through to two hundred. Ma Ponk said I didn't pick fast enough and some of the other older workers said I didn't get enough dew cotton in my sack. Ma Ponk considered a heavy dew a blessing from God, because wet cotton packed tightly together and weighed more. For years, I had watched as she and the others found their favorite sacks, chose the best rows and, in spite of the possibility of getting soaked with dew, started immediately to pull the wet cotton from the bolls and fill their sacks.

For some reason, however, I could never quite manage to be at full steam when competing with an early morning dew. I just didn't like getting wet. It slowed me down. So I'd stand or sit on the turn road by the trailer until the sun had dried some of the dew.

One morning while sitting on the turn road, I'd fastened my eyes on Cooter Man, a real cotton picker. Cooter Man was not his real name, but we all called him that. He could pick a bunch of cotton and everyone knew it. In a day, he had been known to pick more than four hundred pounds. Cotton doesn't weigh much, and four hundred pounds of it is almost a trailer load.

I overheard people saying Cooter Man snapped his cotton. Snapping was not legal except at the end of the season. Authorized snapping allowed the field hand to pick both the boll and the scraps of cotton that had been left behind. But to snap at the beginning of the season when all the bolls were full was not acceptable, especially if you got caught. Cooter Man had a reputation in both the white and the colored communities for speaking his mind and backing it up with physical activity. A man with his reputation never quite got caught snapping at the wrong time. Like the others, I didn't say anything to Cooter about his snapping, but I had my opinion. I figured he snapped.

I watched as Cooter Man swaggered from the truck to the field. He finished his smoke, put his sack over his shoulder, stood up, looked around and said, "See y'all at the end." Cooter Man was fast. Not one to be hampered by dew or rules, he straddled his rows, bent down, and all you could see were arms tossing cotton into a sack. Within minutes, Cooter Man was well on his way to beating his own record. As I watched, I knew that I'd be doing well if I ever picked two hundred pounds.

"Boy, don't stay on the end forever!" Ma Ponk yelled.

"Yes'm, I'm getting ready to start now."

It was easy to find my two rows. They were the only ones with cotton. The rows on either side of me had been started much earlier, leaving me the late starter and the one not likely to pick two hundred pounds. As I put the cotton-sack strap over my head, I reluctantly began to hum and slowly pick the cotton from the bolls. Looking down those mile-long rows, all I could think about was the cotton gin. I didn't want to pick cotton; I wanted to work at the Lake Washington or Wildwood gin.

For years, the gins had been key places for colored employment. In fact, a cotton gin was considered by many people as the ideal place to work. Uncle Johnny worked at the Lake Washington gin and he had promised that he'd help me get on, but vacancies rarely, if ever, came open. Just the other day, I had heard them talking about the gin and naming the lucky ones that had gotten hired. Needless to say, I was only given a promise, but I hoped it would soon materialize. As I continued to pick wet cotton which was drying out by now, my mind kept straying to the gins.

I had stood across the road from the cotton gin by the lake the Saturday before and watched as the colored men and boys with their sling blades and rakes cut the grass from around that massive tin structure. Throughout the gin, men could be seen greasing the many wheels and pulleys. I stood there envious of their laughter and their jokes as they made ready for the first trailers of cotton to pull in. The sun shone brightly on the massive tin roof. I just stood silently wishful, watching the colored men with bare backs and rippling muscles laughing and joking with each other as they moved the old trailers from last year out of the way. I wanted to be with them, but if I didn't get any help from Uncle Johnny, I'd go another summer working in the cotton fields instead.

Thinking about working at the gin must have added speed to my efforts. My sack was about one-fourth full and with any luck at all, I'd be able to weigh in about seventy-five or eighty pounds of cotton. I didn't have much dew cotton, but my sack had begun to drag heavy. If no one bothered me for some candy, I might be able to achieve my goal of two hundred pounds.

I hated selling candy, but it was my mother's way to earn extra money and trade for the bed linens she wanted. Whether I wanted to or not, my mother would load me down with boxes of cheap candy consigned to her by the white "candy man." No one really knew the candy man, but like clockwork, at the beginning of the chopping-and-picking-cotton seasons, he'd show up. He would have his 1954 Chevrolet piled high with boxes of candy, cheap sheets, red-letter Bibles and cotton print dresses that were never true to their sizes.

No one ever called him by his name. He was just the candy man. Segregation didn't bother him. On a hot dusty day, he'd step right into your house, get himself a drink of water and even eat if food was offered. Every Wednesday evening and Saturday morning, he came to Glen Allan and drove straight to the colored section. When his car appeared on our streets, the smaller colored kids would come running. As he drove slowly and purposely through our section, scores of little barefoot colored children would run alongside his car. Occasionally he'd toss out a few pieces of candy which generated squeals of delight and scuffling. He'd slow down to watch the scuffle, already knowing that he had not given enough for everyone. Then he just drove slowly on down the road, laughing all the way.

He sold only to the colored women and they knew him to be cheating them blind, but his business opportunity was their only chance to barter for the extras they needed. He had uncovered a gold mine, and my mother was among the many colored women who insured his mine.

Mama lived at the very end of the colored section, right across from the colored school. By the time he got to her house the candy man would be almost out of candy, but my mother was one of his good accounts, so he always held her boxes out. My brother Claiborne and my sisters Claudette, Clara and Carolyn would all be outside waiting for his car. His car would be loaded with cheap but brightly colored wares. He stopped and spoke to each of us by name before he opened the trunk. We stood and ogled the pretty things we saw.

Loaded down with more boxes of candy to be sold that week, each of us walked behind Mama as she opened the old screen door that led into the front room, which doubled as a bedroom. Mama loved sheets and had sold enough candy the week before to get a new set. She was happy. The candy man was happy. We watched from the front window as he lit his pipe, folded his money and drove away.

My sack of cotton was getting heavier. I figured that if I could weigh my first sack in before nine and it was eighty pounds I could get my two hundred pounds today. It was too early to sell candy, so no one had broken my stride. I had been so preoccupied with thinking about wanting to work at the gin and my dislike of selling candy that my sack was completely filled before I noticed it. It felt like almost eighty pounds to me, and the scales confirmed my guess. My first sack of cotton weighed more than seventy-five pounds. With this encouragement, I went on to follow the lead set by Cooter Man. I snapped a little and picked a lot. And by the end of the day, I had picked two hundred one pounds of cotton. I was the talk of the field. Ma Ponk could now hold her head high. I really wasn't lazy after all.

The day was finally over. Cooter Man had picked more than four hundred pounds of cotton, and I had reached my goal. It was a sweet ride home. In those days, we felt cotton would be king forever, and if we were to survive, it would be necessary to successfully master the task of picking cotton. That day, I had earned my badge.

As the field truck made its way back to Glen Allan, I sat on the back with my friends, laughing, joking and discussing the events of the day. And now only one thing more could make me happier — to stop at the Lake Washington gin. After all, I was a good field hand now. Ma Ponk gave me her permission after I assured her that I would be coming home with Uncle Johnny. Mr. Walter agreed to stop and let me off the truck, so in a few minutes, I found myself walking with pride up the well-traveled dirt road to the Lake Washington gin.

I could hear the joking and laughter of the gin workers as they labored together to pull the cotton trailers into position. They all seemed to have so much fun while sitting atop the trailers piled high with cotton. As I got closer to the gin all I could see were young men both white and colored, laughing as they worked, their bare backs and dirty blue jeans wet from summer sweat. Together, they were pushing trailers loaded with the day's pick of cotton. I could hardly wait. This is what I had been waiting for, the opportunity to work side by side with the really tough guys.

I knew the colored guys well. Hurley, Ben, and Sonnyman were there. Bubba was there, with his curly hair matted to his head from sweat. I didn't know many of the white guys, because some of them were from around the lake. Most of the white sharecroppers from around the lake didn't speak to colored people. Today, though, it didn't matter. Armed with my new hard-earned reputation, I walked up to them as if I were part of the group.

They stood among trailer loads of cotton that had come in from the surrounding fields. They were busy, colored and white guys working together, getting all those trailers in line according to plantation. This didn't stop me. I immediately began to tell them about my day. I told them how I had managed to take a small lesson from Cooter Man and snap a little while picking, and that at the end of the day, I had picked more than two hundred pounds of cotton. They listened as they worked, and even moved aside so I could join them. I started to take off my field shirt and tie it around my waist. Then I saw their muscles — so many more than I had. I kept my shirt on, but I joined the guys at the gin as they pushed the trailers of cotton around.

We pushed and pulled. We laughed and talked, never getting too friendly with the white guys, but getting friendly enough. While we were busy lining the trailers up, I heard the roar and screech of tractors. The other guys looked up and quickly moved to the other side or jumped into the trailers. This was new to me; I just stood there. But within seconds, I knew why they scrambled and I, too, ran for cover. The tractors were being driven by the sons of the white farmers, who did most of their own work. Their faces and backs had been burned by the sun. They too were sweaty and smelly, but they enjoyed the cool breeze that had begun to flow from the lake. Part of their fun was driving their tractors and trailers at an accelerated speed, stopping within an inch of our lives.

All this activity and excitement necessitated the use of the bathroom. There was none, however, so all of us peed on the north side of the tin building. We didn't talk, we just peed and watched as the streams of urine hit the hot tin and dried. Then we all ran back to the front of the gin. The tractor drivers jumped on their tractors now that their trailers were unhooked, and sped off, with rocks and gravel flying everywhere. They drove back to their world, and the rest of us stayed in ours.

By now the shift was about over, and Uncle Johnny would be ready to leave. I waited until all the cotton-loaded trailers were covered with tarps in case it rained. While the workers were doing this, I walked over to the loading dock and watched Ben sweep the floors. Boy, I told myself, how I wish I had his job! He didn't have many muscles, but like the other gin workers, he had his shirt off and tied around his waist. We talked for a while until I heard Uncle Johnny calling me. It had been a great day — all I could ask.

I never did get to work at the gin, but I continued to chop and pick cotton until my junior year in high school, when I got the job of my young life, as the utility boy at Hilton Food Store.

Even though the white and colored boys played together in the fields, we rarely spoke or related to each other socially. There was an exception, however, that stands out as one of the warm memories of my childhood.

It was during the cotton-picking season that we always went to help Mr. Jennings, a small white farmer, finish his crop. Going to Mr. Jennings' was fun because his two teenage boys, Billy and Jim, were very friendly. Billy and I would pick cotton side by side. Even though he was older, we would wrestle and he'd let me win. Mr. Jennings couldn't afford a whole crew of field hands, so he would pick up Ma Ponk and me and a few others in his car. When we got to his home, his wife had our cotton sacks ready. While the adults were talking, I would be watching Mr. Jennings' back screen door for Billy. He was always late, but his father made him pick cotton and work alongside us.

Being small, I used a handmade sack, and I picked cotton off Billy's row. We laughed and played until about midmorning, when it was time for him to go get the trailer ready to weigh the cotton. When Billy quit, Ma Ponk let me stop. Billy and I would sit on the shady side of the trailer and prepare to sleep until the first field hand was ready to have his sack of cotton weighed.

One day, while Billy and I were midway up the field in an area called the clearing, his girl friend came to see him. There I was, right in the middle of a cotton-field romance. They didn't do much talking. I recall that Billy stood up and pulled her close to him and they walked around to the opposite end of the cotton trailer where nobody could see them. Billy told me to climb on top of the trailer and watch and to call him if I saw anyone coming, especially his father. This was my first encounter with teenage love, and I didn't know what to think. So I didn't think, I just watched for his father. I was part of a secret. I didn't see anyone coming, but when I finally turned around and leaned over the edge of the trailer, I saw Billy and his girl hugging and kissing. Billy looked up at me and laughed. The girl must not have thought it was funny, because she took off running through the field. At the end of the day, Billy drove us home. As I got out of the car, Billy winked and I laughed. The secret was safe.

Today, most of the cotton gins near my hometown are relics of a past life. The once popular Wildwood gin is idle now, the structures fallen down. A few tin smoke stacks remain. Johnson grass, buttercups and even wild mint grow around and through the buildings. A few broken-down wooden trailers, pieces of rotten cotton sacks, and rusty parts of old scales lie silently on the ground amidst the debris, reminders now of the activity that once made the gins my ideal place to work.

Very few people chop cotton anymore. New herbicides and various types of chemical agents to kill grass have almost completely eliminated the need for physical labor. And very few people pick cotton anymore. The mechanical cotton picker, which has been expanded and developed more each year, has almost totally replaced the human cotton picker I used to know. The industrialization of the rural South played a great part in changing our life-style, and it happened about the same time as the now-famous civil-rights struggle of the 1960s began. These two changes brought an abrupt end to an era — the colored era in which I grew to adulthood, like my parents and grandparents and great-grandparents before me.

Chapter Eleven

Dreams, Trains and Other Things

Mrs. Jeffries owned Wildwood Plantation where Ma Ponk and I, together with several others, spent our summers chopping cotton. To Ma Ponk, chopping cotton at Wildwood was a way of life. To me, it was an ordeal. The ritual hardly ever changed. She and I would start our days with the crowing of the roosters and the barking of the dogs. Ma Ponk was always one to get up quickly without much fuss, whereas I faced each morning as a major challenge. While she would get our breakfast, I would have the job of emptying our portable toilets, commonly called slop jars. Emptying the slop jars and starting the morning fire were my jobs. And if we were to be ready for Mr. Walter's field truck, all those jobs had to be done quickly.

By the time the fire was hot and the kitchen stove ready, Ma Ponk would be completely dressed for the fields. We ate breakfast on the run — drip Maxwell House coffee, fried sausages and hot hoecakes. Then I would stand on the front porch as a signal to Mr. Walter that we were ready.

I could hear Mr. Walter's truck coming down the gravel road, the honking of the horn and the sound of Mr. Walter calling out, "Git up! Git out! You gonna work today." As in the many summers before, Ma Ponk got in the cab of the truck while I climbed onto the back, stepping over half-asleep field hands and tubs filled with ice and soda pop.

Surrounded by flies and bloodthirsty mosquitoes, I kept quiet and listened to gossip I shouldn't have heard. The back of the truck now filled to capacity, and we all rocked along to Wildwood for another long hot summer day.

It was July, the month of long hot days, but July also had a good feature. It was the month our relatives and friends came home to visit from up north. Oh, how I remember those well-told Marco Polo stories of a life too good for me to even imagine! Deep within most of our hearts, we harbored the desire to be part of that good life that waited for us all just north of the Mason-Dixon line. Mrs. Jeffries' Wildwood Plantation was too big to be handled entirely by her tenants, so during the peak of the summer, the hot month of July, she would have her straw boss hire extra hands to ensure that the young cotton plants were properly weeded. For me, this was a bittersweet situation — bitter in that I would be chopping cotton, but sweet in that Mrs. Jeffries' fields were next to the highway and I could see firsthand the shiny new cars or the rare sight of cabs bringing those northern visitors home.

It was cars and cabs from Greenville, Mississippi, now, because the train didn't come to Glen Allan anymore. According to the old folk, the Illinois Central Railroad used to back into Glen Allan, but now Greenville was our closest connection. For years, the decaying tracks by the colored cemetery were the only reminder of this mechanical caravan that carried dreamers North to a land of promise. The old Union Station had long since decayed, and only the memory of the old folk kept that era of the train alive.

Standing on my designated cotton row with my wide-brim cowboy hat partially shading my face because I didn't want to get any darker, I was now ready to chop as little as I could and watch the road as much as I could. However, the straw boss was determined that my back would stay bent. Mrs. Jeffries had a straw boss known for having a rather mean disposition, and we colored field hands were his stepping-stones to white respectability. As I remember bits of field conversation, straw bosses were usually from the poor white families who were tolerated but never liked by other whites. If it were not for their color, our social and economic conditions would have been equal. Ma Ponk called them "po' red-necks tryin' to be white."

"Look at 'im chewing on dat cigar and acting like he's kin to Miss Jeffries. Well, he ain't. He's jus po' white trash. I know his ma and pa. His pa just about grew up on my ma's cooking. Now he's too proud to stoop inside her door. I wouldn't give you a plug nickel for a po-butt straw boss."

And Ma Ponk, knowing how I liked to look at cars rather than chop cotton, always tried to shield me from the watching eyes of the boss. I can't blame my encounter with the straw boss on Ma Ponk, because she always did her best to teach me how not to incur his anger.

"You never know when he's coming. He's sneaky, and always trying to catch you ratting on the job," she would caution.

Naturally, I took advantage of his absence, but I kept my ears trained to listen for his truck and the meanness of his voice. While the other field hands were getting ready to start their day, I took off to the bushes, the field name for nature's toilet. Apparently I had been gone too long, because while I was answering nature's call, I heard his truck. I saw the dust flying and I heard Ma Ponk angrily calling my name. I was too slow, she was too late and the straw boss was on time. I tried to get lost in the cloud of dust from his truck, but he saw me anyway.

"Hey, boy, ain't you Elna's? The day ain't even started and here you are going to s —. Boy, you niggers'll do anythang to keep from giving us a good day's work. Well, go on, git down there to your row."

As I walked quickly to my row beside Ma Ponk who had kept up my row by chopping the weeds from both, the straw boss walked over and started to talk with her.

There he stood with a fixed frown, talking to Ma Ponk as she kept right on chopping. He wore a used plantation hat, a neatly pressed khaki outfit with a red bandanna at the neck, and black boots. He had a half-smoked cigar hanging out of his mouth, and he didn't look directly at Ma Ponk while he was talking to her, but studied the clouds.

"Elna, how you this morning? Thank we gonna have a good crop this year?"

"Yes, sir," Ma Ponk answered, not looking up. "Yes, sir, I wuz jus telling my boy here how you sho brought in a good crop last year."

Undeserved praise, the conversation used by all the field hands to defuse the straw boss' meanness, always worked. As he puffed rings of smoke over our heads, still looking at the clouds, he agreed with Ma Ponk.

"Yeah, Elna, we did do a good job last year. Well, I'd better git now. You keep track of that young 'un."

Ma Ponk finally stood up and stretched as we watched his truck make a new cloud of dust. He was gone and the field hands could relax.

"You gotta make him thank he done something," Ma Ponk said. "But I know his mama. They ain't got a house as decent as mine."

With the straw boss gone and Mr. Walter in control, I could start watching for my Uncle William Henry and Aunt Dora from Chicago. I knew every car in Glen Allan, so it would be easy for me to spot a new car loaded with well-dressed colored people. I could hardly wait to see them. I thought they were all rich, because I'd get fifty cents to polish one pair of their shoes. I was in awe of the northern visitors. Their clothing was extra nice. Men wore suits in the middle of the week and their hair would be pressed to their heads, held in place at night by stocking caps. And the women wore pants! Pedal pushers, wide-brimmed straw hats and dark glasses, just like the movies. And their cars were models not seen every day in our town.

This July, however, was even more important than most. Not only was Uncle William Henry coming home, but Melvin was coming home too. It had been nearly twenty years since he had left by train, and he had not returned. Now he was coming to Greenville. Once there, he would take a cab to Glen Allan. A cab was a rare sight in Glen Allan. Usually, only white people took cabs, and not too often. I had never seen Melvin. He was Ma Ponk's youngest son. Everyone was happy for her, and we could hardly wait for his visit. We wanted him to tell us about the good life in Detroit. As I chopped I watched the road. I wanted to be the first to see the cab speeding past Wildwood, headed to Glen Allan.

After our traditional hour off for lunch, I reluctantly left the shade of the big oak trees and joined the other field hands, walking back to pick up where we had stopped. The smell of sardines, crackers, moon pies and cold chicken was gone now, lost in the ever-present smell of weed killer. I took my chopping position again, with my eyes firmly on the highway.

My determination paid off.

"Ma Ponk, he's here! He's here! There go the cab!"

Ma Ponk stood up and watched the cab go by. Her boy Melvin had come home. I couldn't wait to meet this new older cousin. I wanted to meet him first so I could be the favorite one. I wanted to show him around Glen Allan, to be near this visitor from the alien and magical North. The end of the day finally came. The old green field truck with its large canvas top was filled to capacity. No one was asleep now. We were all anxious to get home, and no one more anxious than Ma Ponk and me. Even though it was a weekday, Ma Ponk would let me dress up and wear my short blue pants and my yellow puckered nylon shirt. I had to make sure my legs and face were greased and my hair combed.

He was there, this tall stranger, standing inside the gate waiting on us. Golden brown with curly hair, dressed in an off-white suit, there he stood with long outstretched arms, waiting for his mother. It didn't matter why he had waited so long to come home. He was in Glen Allan now, and that was all that mattered.

Melvin spent only four days in Glen Allan. During those days he recounted for us his adventures of the past twenty years. I took him around the colored section of Glen Allan, and he went uptown to say hello to Mrs. Knight, the white seamstress that we all knew. His trip was short, but he promised he would not stay away that long again. Sunday came quickly, and all too soon it was time for him to leave. Ma Ponk cried, I cried, Aunt Willie Mae cried and Melvin cried, as he stood waiting for the cab with his two suitcases in hand. When the cab came and he got in, we all started crying again. We waved and waved until the cab was out of sight. Melvin would be catching the Illinois Central from Greenville to Memphis and from there to Detroit.

That summer would see a number of northern visitors and they would always keep my head filled with dreams of life in a land where color bars were non-existent and colored people could eat in the same places with whites.

The joyous visits from our northern cousins were sometimes returned. During the winter when all the field work was complete, Aunt Willie Mae, Ma Ponk's younger sister, would go to Saginaw to visit Mamie and Roy. Ma Mae had told us all that summer that she would be spending two to three weeks with her daughter. We were all happy about her upcoming trip, but there was also some sadness. If she left, would she come back? The Illinois Central carried away many more people than it ever returned.

The day finally arrived when it was time for Ma Mae's annual visit. We were all excited, because we'd get the chance to ride to Greenville and wait at the train station with her. For these trips, the colored women usually wore their best, and Ma Mae was no exception. She always wore her blue wool suit. She would painstakingly apply makeup to her light olive complexion and pile her long black hair into a ball at the back of her head. With her face partially veiled and her suitcases packed, she was ready to head north. According to Ma Mae she would ride the Illinois Central north to Memphis where she would change trains. Once the train was out of Memphis, there were no Jim Crow laws and she could sit wherever she pleased. Ma Ponk made sure Ma Mae had packed a good lunch of fried chicken and plain buttermilk-cake slices. She needed the light lunch because the dining car would not be open to her until much later, past Memphis.

I was so happy about Mae getting to go to Saginaw that you'd think I was the one going north. We'd always leave early for Greenville, because Poppa was going to drive. He was very slow, and his '49 Buick rarely made the complete twenty-seven-mile trip without breaking down. Aunt Willie Mae and I would sit in the back, since Ma Ponk sat on the passenger side up front to give Poppa directions. Aunt Willie Mae, with two hours to get there, would always be nervous because she didn't want to miss the train. You see, she had written to her daughter, Mamie, and she had to make sure she got to Saginaw on time.

We'd get there with plenty of time to spare, and the Union Station would be packed on both the colored and the white sides. I never really knew what happened on the white side of the station, but I will always remember the side which was a part of my life. Colored men and women in their Sunday best lined the walls to the ticket cage, buying one-way tickets north. Their worn suitcases were held together with leather belts and neckties, and they were weighted down with brown paper bag lunches. Their eyes would be bright as light bulbs, while their relatives would be crying as if the train were taking the loved ones to those eternal green pastures. Some who were departing would cry too. I don't know if the tears were for joy, because now they had a chance to go north and be somebody, or for fear that once they boarded the old Illinois Central, they might never return again. I have found that fear to be justified. Many of the colored passengers never returned home again.

The whistle could be heard about a quarter of a mile from Greenville, and the ticket agent would make his last call. Aunt Willie Mae and the others departing Greenville would all get up together and go to the back of the loading zone assigned to the coloreds. Even though we weren't going anywhere, we went too.

"Git back, y'all, git back, the train gotta have room!" yelled the cigar-smoking track man who guided the train to a halt. As if God had spoken, we quickly moved back past the concrete walk to the area between the walk and the building. We watched as the train unloaded, and we listened as the colored porter gave us additional instructions.

Being a porter on a train was a good job in those days, and the colored porter was just as important to the colored traveler as the conductor was to the train. When I grew up, I thought, I might want to be a porter. The porter seemed to represent the best in colored. His shoes were highly polished, and his white shirt, stiffer than a board, stood out elegantly against his black suit furnished by the railroad. We called him Mister as he looked at his gold watch and assured us (our private conductor, you might say) the train would be leaving on time. He would make his way to Ma Ponk because she knew him. She had been a train rider for many years. According to her, only the poor coloreds rode the bus. Ma Ponk introduced the porter to her sister and made him swear that after the whites had been served, he'd slip her some hot coffee and get her a pillow without charging. Of course he said yes. How could he, our conductor, say no with so great a cloud of witnesses?

Everyone getting off the train seemed to have found the dream. Colored men in striped suits and beaver hats carried matched luggage beside beautiful colored ladies with amber rouged faces and red lips. The ladies' hair was pressed to their heads and clusters curled at the back or side. They wore brightly colored dresses and carried coats with bits of fur. They said "Pardon me" as they whisked by with their train cases in their hands. They quickly walked to the colored side of the station, but with the air of "I am only doing this to keep these red-necks happy. Why, in Chicago, there's no such thing as separate."

The white conductor made his call, "All aboard!" Aunt Willie Mae was among the first to climb on the train. She wanted to get a seat near the window so she could wave. Ma Ponk was crying and waving not knowing if Aunt Willie Mae would be back.

After the train was out of sight, we all returned to Poppa's car. Ma Ponk was at ease because she knew the porter would take care of her sister. Before leaving Greenville for Glen Allan, we stopped by the pastry shop and picked up some hot French bread. As we headed the '49 Buick back down Number 1 highway to Glen Allan I fell asleep, dreaming that maybe one day I'd be boarding that same train heading north.

As the autumns and winters passed, I spent many more hot summers enduring the rocky rides in Mr. Walter's truck, eating sardines with crackers, and watching out for the straw bosses. Ma Ponk and I had been a team for most of my life. She had taught me how to work and how to survive in our colored environment. But she had also shown me the value of an education. I knew that her younger son Sidney had returned from the war, entered college and later received his doctorate. She could not change her lot in life, but she was profoundly affecting the lives of those of us who were blessed to have passed her way.

I thought surely I'd spend the rest of my days, at least through high school, working in the fields, because any other job for a high school boy was held for the whites. But as fate would have it, two summers before I graduated, I was hired to work for Hilton's Food Store, a job I will always remember. This job helped me keep my dreams intact and achieve that all-important goal, graduation from high school.

Even today when I return to Mississippi, older colored people remember me as the boy who carried their sacks or cut their meat.

I wanted the job at the town's biggest grocery store more than I had ever wanted anything but I just knew I wouldn't get it because a number of white boys had applied for the job. If I got that job, it would mean I didn't have to chop cotton during the summer. I would make a couple of dollars more per hour and have a part-time job while I was in high school. The owner of the store had seen me work on Saturdays at the local post office, oiling the floor, and he asked the postmistress about me. I had a reputation for being a good worker, probably because I always said "Yes, sir" and "No, ma'am" to the town's whites. They thrived on that. After getting up the nerve to apply for a job that was normally reserved for white boys, I anxiously waited day in and day out, wishing and hoping, knowing deep in my heart that I'd never get that job.

I was on my knees scrubbing away at the old post office floor when the store owner walked in. Towering over me and looking down on my crouched frame, he told me I was some lucky kid, that he was going to give me a chance to work in his store. The news almost caused a coronary arrest. I was so excited that I finished cleaning and polishing the post office floors in record time.

When I left the post office after having earned a dollar and a half, I ran down to the back of Glen Allan as fast as my legs could carry me. I can't remember touching the wobbly steps as I ran into the kitchen to tell my mother. When I told her, she just raised her hands and said, "My God can do anything." It had to be God. White people weren't known for their generosity towards blacks in those days. I ran out the back door and over to Ma Ponk's house. Breathlessly, I repeated my story to her, and she just beamed. This was something to be proud about. I had been given a chance to do a white man's job.

I was going to start work Monday after school. By Sunday, every black person in Glen Allan knew I had gotten a decent job. Why, this could last me all my life and I'd never have to work the fields again! The knowledge caused great rejoicing.

Monday afternoon seemed a long time in coming, and the old yellow school bus seemed slower than ever. I just couldn't be late my first day. Whites said we were never on time, and I had promised God and a couple of other people that I'd really do my best to hold that good job down. After going to nearly every plantation between Greenville and Glen Allan, the bus finally got to my house. I leaped off before it reached a complete stop. Ma Ponk had a sandwich waiting and a number-three tub of hot water. I had to take a bath and load up on Mum deodorant because I couldn't go around white folks smelling.

When I got to the store, I was shown around and given my list of duties. It was a long list, but I didn't mind. I was going to do a good job if it killed me. I worked hard, never stopping except to go outside to use the colored john. I worked so well that I surprised not only them, but also myself. I soon learned to cut meat and package and sell it, and could I say "Yes, ma'am"! I had *manners*.

While working there, I met a couple of white boys who were the sons of plantation owners. They'd come by the store nearly every Saturday in their light beige Corvair, and we'd laugh and talk about sports and girls. During the summer months, they'd come by nearly every day when I wasn't busy, and we'd almost forgotten that we were doing a forbidden thing. We had begun to talk together about our girl friends, swap lies and trade pictures, and when a white boy went that far, you had better believe he was breaking tradition.

Then it happened. One day they asked me to go out with them, and that was a social taboo. My boss called me aside and encouraged me to remember that I was colored and they were white. They stopped coming in the store so often and finally quit altogether. I don't know what happened to the guys, but for awhile we almost became friends.

I worked in that same store all through high school and made a number of other friends, but nothing was the same after that summer.

Even though the white high school was only blocks from where I lived, I traveled more than one hundred miles round trip each day to the colored high school in Greenville. We had begun to hear about integration, but it was very difficult to imagine. As the winters and summers went by, I worked hard in the fields, in school, and at the food store, knowing that one day I might have my chance to go north.

At last I came to the end of my high school years. I would soon be graduating, and I could hardly wait. Everyone was happy, but no one more than I. As my graduation drew closer, I found myself running all over Glen Allan delivering invitations. Seeing my name in official print on my graduation invitation was one of the highlights of my life. Not only did I cover the colored section of Glen Allan, but there were selected whites who also received an invitation. In spite of the segregated life-style, there were those few southern whites who lived beyond the limits of bigotry. And while growing up in Glen Allan, I encountered such a person — Mrs. Knight, the town's seamstress.

Even though she was related to major plantation owners and recognized as such, she nevertheless responded to all people with a genuine sense of warmth. She had always encouraged my educational pursuits and was most interested in my college endeavor. Even though I raked leaves for her on Saturdays, I was never made to feel as if I had landed a permanent position. She always spoke of a brighter future and the value of an education.

I remember one Saturday morning many years ago when I ran uptown to Mrs. Knight's to rake leaves. My step-grandmother Ida had gotten me the job. Even though Mrs. Knight wanted every leaf raked and bagged — a difficult task — I always looked forward to my work and to waiting for her at the shop.

The shop, a small white one-room building on the south side of her home, was filled with unfinished dresses and bolts of half-used materials. Even though it was extremely crowded and in disarray, even though she was partially blind, she knew the location of everyone's order. She was a rather short, plump lady with piles of white hair pulled up into a bun on top of her head. And she moved with a tremendous amount of nervous energy. She walked fast, she talked fast and she was always busy.

In spite of her age and eyesight, her sewing never suffered — nor did her yard upkeep. With the quickness of a younger woman, Mrs. Knight would take me out to her big yard and point out the bushels of fig leaves that had fallen during the week. I was expected to see that each leaf was bagged. Her home was uptown and although it was not a typical southern mansion, it was nonetheless a house of substance, a fact which required the yard to be almost immaculate.

Before I worked for Mrs. Knight, her yard had been cared for by a seventy-five-year-old colored man we called "Mr. Antiseptic." He had developed a reputation for keeping yards the very best, and this was the man of experience whom I had to follow. "Do it right the first time" was Mrs. Knight's working motto, and I guess she had been giving that advice for years.

"Come on, Cliff-tin, let's get this over 'fore the sun comes out."

Putting on her glasses and adjusting her shoulder shawl over her nearly floor-length dress, she'd walk with me to the back of the shop, to her toolshed, where I'd get the rake, the wheelbarrow and a couple of gunnysacks. After pointing out the millions of fallen leaves, she'd hurry back to her shop, where customers would be waiting, and I would start the task before me.

The task seemed endless. The leaves never stopped falling from the big southern fig trees. Even as I raked they continued to come down all around me. However, after about two hours of work, I could begin to see progress. The gunnysacks were filling up, and my stomach was calling for food. Fortunately for me, it was close to lunchtime.

"Cliff-tin, Cliff-tin, come on. Let's eat lunch," Mrs. Knight called as she hurried from her shop, walking through the heavy wrought-iron gates to her home.

As Mrs. Knight hurried, I dropped the rake, ran to wash my hands, and walked fast to catch up. We'd both go through her antique-filled living room into her breakfast room, where we would both sit at the same table and eat.

Leftover stewed chicken, hard wheat bread and slightly warmed lima beans made up our meal. There we sat together, separated by more than six decades and the colors of our skin. There was not much conversation, but just enough. After we finished, we both left the quietness and returned to our respective jobs.

Now that I was graduating from high school, I especially wanted to give Mrs. Knight an invitation. She met me at the door and, when I handed her the invitation, squealed with delight. I knew I would always cherish this relationship. In a day when coloreds used the back door and never gave any thought to the possibility of eating with whites, we had forged a friendship that defied the times.

With all the invitations out and the day drawing closer, my fears mounted. What would I really do? Would I leave Glen Allan? Where would I go to college? There was no money. Would I get a scholarship? These fears I hid in my heart as I anticipated graduation day.

On a warm night in May 1963 I graduated as the valedictorian of my class. Nearly all of the Glen Allan coloreds had come to Greenville to watch their sons and daughters receive their diplomas. The high school gym was packed. As the music cued us to march in, out of the corner of my eye I saw my mother smiling through tears. There beside her sat Ma Ponk, quietly dignified with her arms folded, slightly rocking back and forth. She had raised me. She had done her job.

As valedictorian, I was required to make the valedictory address. I was nervous — perhaps more nervous than I had ever been in my life. With the colored principal behind me and the platform filled with white representatives from the Western Line School District, I slowly walked to the podium and began my speech.

"We can't see into our future but we know it holds promises."

I spoke to my graduating class, our parents and friends in the open gym at O'Bannon High School, which that night was transformed into an arena of expectations, a place where for many of us, our futures would begin. As my shaky voice echoed through the gym, usually filled with shouting crowds cheering the basketball teams to victory, I realized that this night, more than any other night in my life, would mark a change in my destiny.

After I spoke the diplomas were awarded. At last the principal, Mr. A. T. Williams, called my name — 1963 honor graduate, Clifton Lemoure Taulbert. I remembered my training and managed to leave my seat and walk across the stage as planned. With tears welling in my eyes, I received my cherished certificate of completion and went back to my seat.

That warm southern night in May 1963 did indeed end an era in my life. Until then, I had lived a life-style that had evolved after the Emancipation Proclamation. Little did I know that my life, as well as the lives of millions of southern colored Americans, would change drastically during the revolutionary '60s. A completely new set of expectations would be developed, as well as a new vocabulary more descriptive of the reality of our people.

As the excitement of graduation waned, I was faced with the challenge of the next step. Even though I was the honor graduate, I received no college scholarship. The scholarships given to O'Bannon graduates went to the football and basketball stars. My next step started with an invitation to stay with relatives in Saint Louis, an invitation I gladly accepted. I was not sure what I'd do in such a city, but I knew Glen Allan could no longer be my home. My dreams and ambitions stretched far beyond the resources of a small southern town. Determined to look for work and eventually go to college, I began to prepare for my trip north.

The year of my graduation, the faithful Illinois Central Railroad that had come to Greenville for as long as I could remember made a heartbreaking announcement — the train would soon cease "servicing Greenville." This decision made me among the last to ride the Illinois Central north.

I was to experience a whole world of new challenges at the other end of that train ride. My first challenge was to find a job, and my first job would be washing dishes in a department store restaurant.

I was to experience the civil rights demonstrations of the sixties and learn that even though Saint Louis was considered by us in Mississippi as a northern town, colored people were still having difficult times getting real jobs, meaningful jobs, and contributing to society. I would have to take every opportunity to educate myself, work all day and go to school at night, until I would finally earn my college degree eight years later. I would never be satisfied with what passed for good jobs for colored people, for I knew I was as smart and capable as the whites, and I could never forget the lessons I'd learned growing up in Glen Allan. I couldn't forget the advice I'd heard over and over from Uncle Cleve and Mrs. Knight and others about getting an education and bettering myself. I couldn't forget the ambitions my teachers had for me, and all those times at the colored school when I'd heard about the "big four" colored role models. Most of all, the hopes of my mother, the gentle wisdom of Poppa and the strength and determination of Ma Ponk would remain a part of me as I ventured out of the colored world.

All of this was still a distant dream as I prepared to leave Glen Allan. The date for my departure was set, and arrangements were made for my trip to Greenville. At last the time to leave arrived. All my good-byes were completed, my clothes were packed and I had my train tickets in hand. Not unlike the thousands before me, I carried my packed lunch and listened to Ma Ponk's advice to hide my money in my socks. Ma Ponk not only fixed my lunch of fried chicken sandwiches and sliced buttermilk pound cake, but she made sure I was introduced to the colored porter.

I got to Greenville early so I wouldn't miss my train. They were all there to see me off and keep me encouraged — Ma Ponk; my mother Mary; my brother Claiborne; my sisters

Claudette, Clara, Carolyn and Connie. And I did need their encouragement as I thought about the train. It would be in Metcalfe now, so close to Greenville that we could almost hear it. Suddenly I realized that the train coming through Metcalfe to Greenville was for me, and I began to feel a tinge of fear. As I stood in the colored section of the station with my seventeen-year-old face pressed to the windows, I watched the train in all its puffs of glory appear around the bend and slowly come to a complete stop. My eyes were too misty to really notice those getting off or even those boarding before me. Glen Allan could not make my dreams come true, but it was home, and today I was leaving home for good. I probably would have stood at the window forever except for the call of the conductor, "All aboard, last call!"

As many times as I had seen the train, I had never been inside. I slowly and carefully walked to the colored coach and down the small aisle and found a seat by the window. Looking out, I saw those familiar faces. I waved and cried as I watched my family slowly walk away. I was alone and afraid, trying to be an adult in a train filled with strangers. As the train pulled out of Greenville I wondered about the much talked about transformation that would take place once we crossed the Mason-Dixon line. Would living up north be all that I had dreamed? With the security of family fading out of sight, I clung to the promises I had heard all my life from those who had nurtured me in Glen Allan, once upon a time when we were colored.

ABOUT THE AUTHOR

Clifton Taulbert, an internationally acclaimed speaker, graduated valedictorian from Greenville, Mississippi's O'Bannon High School, served in a classified position with the 89th Presidential Wing of the United States Air Force, and attended the University of Maine and Maryland. Taulbert received his undergraduate degree from Oral Roberts University, and is a graduate of the Southwest Graduate School of Banking at Southern Methodist University.

He is the President of the Freemount Marketing Company of Tulsa, Oklahoma, where he also serves on numerous civic boards and city trusts. He lives with his wife, Barbara Ann, and their two children, Marshall Danzy and Anne Kathryn.

He is also the author of the award-winning book, *The Last Train North*.